Alistair Livingstone joined
Until shortly beforehand, he had never considered policing as a career. Ali went on to make more arrests than any other police officer in the UK and was dubbed 'Supercop' in the media. For Ali, policing wasn't just a job: it was a way of life. After eighteen years of public service, he was devastated to have to resign from the job that he loved as a result of a debilitating and devastating mental breakdown. Against all odds, Ali has recovered to the extent that he has been able to rejoin the police in a role that will enable him to make use of his years of experience.

Broken Blue Line

Alistair Livingstone

ROBINSON

ROBINSON

First published in Great Britain in 2020 by Robinson
This paperback edition published in 2022 by Robinson

1 3 5 7 9 10 8 6 4 2

A CIP catalogue record for this book
is available from the British Library.

ISBN: 978-1-47214-475-1

Typeset in Adobe Garamond Pro by Hewer Text UK Ltd, Edinburgh
Printed and bound in Great Britain by Clays Ltd, Elcograf S.p.A.

Papers used by Robinson are from well-managed forests and other responsible sources.

MIX
Paper from responsible sources
FSC® C104740

Robinson
An imprint of
Little, Brown Book Group
Carmelite House
50 Victoria Embankment
London EC4Y 0DZ

An Hachette UK Company
www.hachette.co.uk

www.littlebrown.co.uk

Dedicated to all the police officers and staff who have held or who are holding the line.
Keep fighting the good fight.

Contents

I

Be careful, he's got a knife

WE ARRIVED AT the outskirts of the town centre, screeching to a halt in the middle of the road. As I scrambled out of my police car, blue lights on and sirens still wailing, there was a scene of panic across the road, with the staff from the takeaway frantically pointing and shouting in the direction of a dark figure now jogging up the road away from us.

'He's tried to attack us. He's got a blade,' said one of the shop workers, breathless and panicky. We'd heard enough. My colleague Stuart and I immediately set off in pursuit of the man.

I shouted after him, 'Police, stand still!' After a quick glance over his shoulder, the suspect accelerated into a sprint and then he was out of sight as he turned down an alleyway. It was around midnight, but the streets were still busy with people heading home from the pubs or making their way to late-night bars and clubs. I drew my Taser from the holster, grasping it in my right hand, and I quickly radioed for more officers to attend the location. 'We've got a runner, he's got a knife, we need more units.'

This was one of those incidents that suddenly escalate unexpectedly and the risk goes through the roof. In all reality, the additional officers would not be just around the corner, so it was going to be down to my colleague and me to get a grip on this and quickly. We hadn't been called to attend an incident involving a knife, or any weapon, in fact; we'd been called to a disturbance at a kebab shop, a very routine call that normally involves trying to reason with a drunk person about something pretty trivial.

As we quickened our pace there were the inevitable questions running through my mind. Who is he? What has actually happened at the shop? Is anyone hurt? I ran down the middle of the road, members of the public standing back, huddling against the walls of shops and buildings.

As I passed one older gent, he said, 'Be careful, he's got a knife,' before quickly getting into a taxi that had just pulled up. That might not seem an especially significant statement, given that we'd already been told about the blade by the shop staff. For me, it was really important information. It meant that despite us having arrived in a blaze of blue-light glory, he still had the knife in his hand and he was certainly not making any effort to hide it from view. It also meant that if some poor unsuspecting member of the public tried to intervene, the chances were that they were going to get stabbed.

As I reached the alleyway the suspect had disappeared into, a thought crossed my mind, *Is he trying to lure us down here? What will happen if we corner him?*

It reminded me of a foot chase many years before in which a colleague had been attacked having chased a suspect down a town-centre alleyway. But we were only a few seconds behind him and there was no time to answer those questions. We'd have to deal with what we found. Even if he did try to attack us with the knife.

I hesitated slightly before swinging to my right and into the darkness; no longer were we under the warm glow of the streetlights. Away from the hustle and bustle of the main road, it was suddenly quiet. As my eyes adjusted to the darkness, I caught a glimpse of him, crouching no more than a few metres ahead of me, tucked behind a wheelie bin. I shattered the silence.

'Show me your hands,' I bellowed, while raising my Taser stun gun in his direction. My tone was aggressive and dominant. Shock and awe was what I was aiming for. Slowly, he began to stand up, looking me dead in the eye. He was calm, really calm. Perhaps he was going to give up and there'd be no confrontation. I turned on the Taser – the torch attached to the weapon illuminating him – and the man was now able to see the red dot dancing around the middle of his chest. Most people know what a Taser can do, and criminals in particular, no doubt, would have paid more attention than most when they were issued to officers a few years earlier. I immediately noticed that he was keeping his hands behind his back, almost as though he had them tucked into his belt. Maybe this was his way of giving up? Or maybe he had the knife in his hand and was preparing to launch himself at me.

I shouted again, 'Show me your hands now or you'll be Tasered.' He showed no reaction or hint of complying. He was becoming more agitated, looking from side to side, trying to work out what his next move would be. Was he going to run? Was he going to fight? Was he going to try to stab us both? Time seemed to stand still.

I stood towering over the suspect, who was someone I'd encountered countless times in various situations; generally they involved him getting nicked. I'd seen the full range of responses from him. On a good day he'd be grumpy but compliant, and on a bad day he'd run and fight. On one occasion he'd decided to spit blood at us before smearing excrement all over his police cell. In truth, he was now a shadow of his former self, but despite the odds being stacked against him he just couldn't quite bring himself to comply. And he still posed a threat, a huge, potentially deadly threat. He was the kind of character that if you gave him an inch he'd take a mile. No more than a minute earlier we had been racing through the town en route to a disturbance at a kebab shop and now we were confronting an armed and potentially very dangerous man. This had gone on long enough – I made a decision.

I squeezed the trigger and shouted, 'Taser, Taser, Taser!' The pop of the Taser firing was followed by the man crying out in pain. The darts from the Taser had hit him in his chest and midriff, and he fell back against the bins, rigid and incapacitated. For the first time I could now see his hands as he fell to the floor, hitting the cold, hard pavement with a thud and a groan. I couldn't see a knife, but that offered little comfort; until we knew otherwise, he still represented an almighty, life-threatening risk. Stuart ran forward while I circled around him, shouting for him to 'Stay down, don't move.' After a brief struggle we had control, his arms pulled tightly behind his back and the handcuffs secured firmly around his wrists; the risk of him stabbing us, or anyone else for that matter, had gone; everything could settle down.

We stood him up.

'Why the fuck did you do that, Livingstone? I haven't got a fucking knife!' he snarled. He seemed to be forgetting the fact that he'd had a blade only moments earlier. He was right, though; when we began to search him, he didn't have a knife. It would turn out that moments before we confronted him, he'd thrown it on top of a flat roof close by. It made me wonder why he had not just complied and shown me his hands. Perhaps he didn't think he'd get Tasered. Or maybe he'd imagined that by stalling us he'd have a chance to work out an unlikely escape. It didn't really matter – he was the only one responsible for what had happened and it was for him to contemplate his actions now, not me.

This was a criminal who was well known to me and my colleagues. A violent house burglar, a robber and a thief who would stoop to incredible depths to fund his unrelenting addiction to Class A drugs. He had been in the grip of that addiction for many years and it had turned him into a violent and dangerous man – unlike most addicts. There wasn't a lot to like about him. It's fair to say that he didn't like me much either as I'd nicked him many, many times; he knew that I was not one for being intimidated by his antics, and now that I'd Tasered him, it probably wouldn't improve our relationship.

After a few minutes, other police officers started arriving and we were able to search him properly and make sure that there was no further risk. He stood silently, but his rage was written all over his face; teeth clenched and breathing deeply. He was clearly not a good loser. Removing the barbs of the Taser was going to be another flashpoint. When the Taser is fired, metal darts penetrate the victim's skin and allow electric current to pass through their body. A bit like a harpoon, each dart has a hook on it to make sure that it doesn't fall out; a little barbaric some may think, but an excellent design feature. Not so great, though, when they need to be taken out of someone's chest! There was no way he was getting in the van with those darts still attached as they'd make a great weapon, so they were definitely coming out.

'Just stay still for a second, I'll be as quick as I can. You'll be OK,' I said to reassure him. I don't think he was very appreciative, particularly as they'd gone a long way in.

Once he was on his way to custody, I returned to my police car, abandoned in the middle of the road, its doors still wide open. Some law-abiding, decent folk had kept an eye on it for us. The street was now a hive of activity with people rushing over to tell us what they had seen. Fortunately, nobody had been stabbed; I think Stuart and I had got there just in the nick of time. It had been a fairly alarming incident for us, so goodness knows how it had felt for the poor shop staff when the attacker had tried to leap the counter with a knife. It was a good reminder that cops need to expect the unexpected, and to be decisive. There's no time to hesitate and there's certainly no time to ponder what to do.

The man was charged with threatening the staff and also being in possession of a knife. He was sent to jail and so the cycle of offending and conviction continued.

When I decided to become a police officer, little did I know just how challenging it would be or how dangerous. I was a normal guy, who was going to be trained and conditioned to tackle some of society's most dangerous and determined criminals. As this incident came to an end, I felt satisfaction and relief. I certainly didn't suspect that within a few years I would be a wreck: shattered, broken, and ready to turn my back on the job that was all I had ever wanted to do. Incidents such as this would change me, permanently.

2

Life before policing

I HAD BEEN A cop for almost two decades: over half my life had been spent in the pressure cooker that is policing. During this time, I had seen a lot of life – the good times, the bad times, the tough times, the fun times and, unfortunately, the desperately sad times. My decision to join the police as a fresh-faced eighteen-year-old straight from school – albeit one with an old head on young shoulders – would change the course of my life for ever.

After two decades of front-line policing, keeping the most vulnerable people safe and tackling some of the most dangerous people in society, the tables turned and it finally broke me. Now I needed help and support as I hit rock bottom. After many months I was still working to restore normality and recover my mental health, but only time would tell if that were possible. On reflection, I've become a much better person for it and I hope that my experience will help others, particularly those who are still charged with keeping the public safe. It is indisputable that there is a huge stigma relating to mental health, and this exists in the police just as it does in society.

For those people who say that they don't 'get' mental health, that's not good enough any more; we all need to understand it.

Looking back over my career, I thought I had a good understanding of it, particularly as I'd encounter mental health issues on a daily basis, but in truth I was massively ignorant. I don't see that as a failing on my part as we can't be experts in everything. Having gone through the experiences I have, though, I'm happy to share them.

I must say from the outset that I am not a great fan of 'survivors' who subsequently proclaim themselves to be experts and want to save the world. I am not an expert. I am just going to share the realities of policing and what happened to me, give you my views on it, and you can take from that what you will. I do, however, hope that my story will help others going through tough times to realise that they're not alone, and that it will raise awareness about the challenges of policing in a modern society and the reality of mental health issues, particularly for police officers.

In the early years, I became accustomed to seeing all that is bad in our society – social injustice, poverty, addiction, violence, death, exploitation and, perhaps most strikingly of all, a lack of compassion. It seemed incomprehensible what some people would do to their fellow human beings; even their own family, friends or colleagues. I often get asked if things are worse now than they were then; put simply, no. We sometimes forget how tough and rough it was back then as well. The gangs and knife crime may be new, but the violence, pressure and constant challenges facing policing certainly aren't.

I had a busy time as a cop, having worked almost exclusively in front-line roles. They say that if you work in a relatively busy place then within seven years you'll deal with everything at least once – a murder, a rape, a suicide, a fatal collision and even the death of a young child. After eighteen years of front-line policing, I'd seen many more than just the one. Ipswich, where I worked, felt like a borough of London at times, but without the might of the Met to call upon, so you have to think fast and hold on for dear life!

I've arrested more than my fair share. I've been threatened by more than my fair share. I've seen more than my fair share of death and destruction. And I've spent more than my fair share of time standing up to bullies and trying to do the right thing. I learned that police officers have to try and make sense of the chaos, and sometimes, no matter how hard you try, that's an impossible task, but it's one that you're expected to complete at the first attempt. I've been a public order tactical advisor, hostage and crisis negotiator, a search advisor and a response sergeant. It was a full-on, operational, life-at-risk world I lived in, with shifts and being on-call too.

Despite all of this, I felt pretty comfortable with it; it may have been exceptionally challenging at times, but I was a round peg in a round hole and loving life. Never in a million years did I expect to become so troubled by the work I was doing that it would mentally break me; and I think the vast majority of the people I worked with thought the same. They used to refer to me as 'a machine' who didn't sleep, lived for the job and just never stopped. Colleagues and the media would refer to me as Super Cop and I became someone that people felt epitomised front-line, operational policing. My job defined me. I felt like I was indestructible and that I would never suffer with any form of ill health, let alone have a mental breakdown. I was Sergeant Ali Livingstone.

It would be fair to say that I never intended to join the police right up until the moment I did. Going through school I was aiming for a career in sport, or perhaps as a paramedic or even the military, but definitely not the police. Unlike many of my colleagues, I had no family history in the police, no relatives who had served as a police officer or police staff, and no direct involvement with the police in any way. At the time, this was quite uncommon, as lots of sons and daughters of serving or retired officers went on to join the job and follow in their families' footsteps.

The hardest part for someone thinking of joining the police is the constant misrepresentation of what cops actually do – if you believed everything you saw on TV, it would be a constant stream of driving offences and fights outside nightclubs. Fortunately, reality is a lot more interesting than that, but the media coverage does cast a significant shadow over the other work that the police deal with: domestic abuse, burglary and theft offences, serious organised crime, terrorism, mental health and safeguarding children, to name just a few. It's one of my biggest frustrations when I hear people, quite innocently and probably subconsciously, belittling the job of the police. It's not just about speeding tickets and dealing with drunks; it's about dealing with some of society's big social issues, working with some of life's most challenging individuals and attending some of the most tragic, challenging and upsetting things you could ever imagine. And yes, occasionally the police issue speeding tickets.

I was very fortunate to have spent the majority of my childhood playing sport to a decent level, and that allowed me to travel the world playing squash, a game I loved. I represented Scotland over eighty times as a junior and captained them at the World Junior Squash Championships in Milan and the Millennium Commonwealth Youth Games in Edinburgh. It was a huge honour and to this day it remains one of my proudest moments. I was born in England but, as my dear grandmother would say, 'You're British by birth but Scottish by the grace of God.'

Without doubt I played my very best squash when representing my country and that was never more apparent than when playing Argentina in the World Championships in 2000. A squash match is the best of five games. I'd won the first game but lost the second, and I was out on my feet. I'd hit the wall, as they say. The court was blisteringly hot and the atmosphere was electric, with the Argentinean team sensing that their man was on the cusp of knocking me, and consequently our team, out of the championships. I remember feeling completely powerless to stop the momentum, but the one thing I'm not is a quitter; I will fight to the very, very end. Gradually I got back into that third game and somehow – I don't know how – I won it and suddenly felt rejuvenated. I came out in the fourth and it was as though nothing could stop me. High on adrenaline, I stormed through the game and won the match. Winning was important, really important, but for me sport is more about what it teaches us. This taught me a great deal. It taught me that no matter how desperate the situation is, you must keep moving forward, inch by inch. No matter how tired you are, you've still got something left, and that 'something' is probably more than you realise. No matter how hopeless you feel, don't give up. Make sure that you leave everything out there; then you can have no regrets.

My squash coach as I grew up was a New Zealander called Mike Penman. He was and still is one of my biggest inspirations. He's a small, slight man who played with his heart on his sleeve and was simply as hard as nails. I can't imagine anyone more fitted to the expression 'It's not the size of the dog in the fight, it's the size of the fight in the dog.' Boy, he has some fight.

I remember he spoke to my mother one morning after we'd been training and he said, 'Ali really needs to toughen up; he's not mentally strong enough and he's too easily upset.' She pointed out that I was still only eleven years old! But Penman was right, kids do need to toughen up. It's part of growing up. How can we expect them to deal with all that life throws at them if they've never had to overcome challenges or difficulties? I owe a huge debt of gratitude to Penman for everything I've achieved in life; a true legend.

My squash also taught me a great deal about the injustice and inequality in the world. At the same World Championships we played the Kenyan team and I spent some time getting to know them over the course of the two weeks we were in Italy. The logistical challenges they'd faced in getting to the championships were almost beyond my comprehension and yet they played their heart and soul out representing their country. They were making the best of what they had; their kit wasn't great and some of them had never had the luxury of top-quality coaching, yet they applied themselves 100 per cent. They did it with grace, respect and humility, in a way I had not seen before in my many years as a junior playing all over the world. It's fair to say that they were one of the weakest teams at the championships in terms of their standard of play, but in many other ways they were the standout performers. It inspired me to make the best of what I have and to be grateful.

Squash is clearly an individual sport. It is not dissimilar to policing, though – we are all individuals and we all contribute in slightly different ways, but we are part of a team, and to be successful we must all put in the effort. I remember the Deputy

Chief Constable once saying during the response to the prostitute murders in Ipswich that the police comprises one big wheel and we are all individual spokes; no spoke is more or less important than another; you need them all. It sounds a bit like 'management speak', but the sentiment is right.

Having finished my A levels, I went to Loughborough University to study Sports Science. By this time I had made up my mind that I wanted to be a police officer, but I had been told that at just eighteen I wouldn't get in, as I lacked life experience, so I'd be wise to do a degree and then apply when I was a bit older. I remember thinking that was a strange concept; I lacked life experience, but by going to university I'd gain that somehow. Uni is not the be all and end all, and I certainly didn't think it would reflect the type of life I'd one day be dealing with in the police. It's a part of life, yes, but some may argue it shelters people from many of the harsher aspects of reality.

I was driven to Loughborough on the Thursday and unpacked my belongings. I got the train back on the Saturday having made my mind up: it was not for me! I did return and stick with it for three months to see if my view changed, but it didn't, I'd made up my mind and I was determined that to gain the life experience expected of me, I needed to do something other than uni. This was a tough decision, as most of my school friends had gone to university and it felt to me as though there was a presumption that it was the done thing. Not only that, but I was acutely aware that I had no job to go back to.

On my arrival back in Ipswich I went to the job centre and successfully applied to Ipswich Hospital to work on one of their help desks. I was now employed for the first time in my life. The role was administrative and involved organising the portering, catering and laundry services in the hospital. It seemed to me to be quite a responsible job, particularly when urgent calls came in needing bloods transferred or collected from the lab. Our team was responsible for getting the right people to the right place at the right time.

One thing the job did show me was just how hard some people have to work for so little. One of the ladies who worked at the hospital had three jobs; she worked as a cleaner in the morning, in our office for most of the day, then as a receptionist in the evening. And she was not alone; there were lots of people holding down several jobs just trying to make ends meet. I was completely shocked. I'd never known anyone who had two jobs, let alone three, and yet this was their life.

Seeing others who are less fortunate made me appreciate what I had, and I don't say that in a condescending or patronising way. I'm full of respect and admiration for them.

I also had to deal with Rose Cottage. That was the name of the hospital mortuary and every day I'd take calls from wards asking for the porters to take someone to Rose Cottage. I remember thinking what a sensitive name it was; in some small way, it may have made a loved one being taken there feel a little less traumatic and a little less final. I had never dealt with death before, I'm not even sure I'd been to a funeral, so this was another valuable lesson, as every one of those calls involved a bereaved family, or so I thought. I very quickly found out that in some cases – quite a number in fact – there was no family at all. It made me contemplate what a lonely world this must be for some people.

I recently came across an interesting tweet in which a guy tells a story about him and his friend taking part in a race. He's an American and he explains that at the side of the road, as they are running along, there is a table with boxes of free bagels for the runners. He says to his friend that they should get a bagel, but his friend says that the queue is too long and it'll take ages to wait. The guy can't believe it – they're free bagels and he really wants one – but the friend doesn't want to waste time and repeats that they shouldn't bother. The guy decides that he's determined to have a bagel, come what may, so he goes to the front of the queue, reaches between two people and grabs a couple of bagels, one for him and one for his friend. Nobody seems to mind that he's not queued up, and he now has the two bagels he was after. This taught him some valuable lessons, he tells us. Some people know what they want, but will come up with reasons why they can't have it. Some people know what they want and will simply go and get it.

I think in many ways he's right: too often people know what they want, but focus instead on all the reasons they can't have it. I was told I was too young, too inexperienced and too naive to join the police, and was persuaded to go to university without even trying first. If you know what you want in life, then find reasons why you can do it, not reasons why you can't.

While working at the hospital I applied to become a special constable, as I felt that would give me a really good insight into the job. I also applied to become a regular police officer at the same time, but presumed I wouldn't be accepted at that point. In the meantime, I'd still be able to gain experience in policing as a 'special'.

One event as a special stands out for me. I was crewed up with a sergeant and we attended the east of Ipswich for reports of some anti-social behaviour. On our arrival it became clear that there had been a stabbing. We found the injured man in the garden of a house with a serious injury to his stomach. I'm not too bad with blood, but it wasn't the most pleasant of sights.

Fortunately, lots of other officers attended and my role became that of guarding the crime scene overnight.

I stood at that scene for hours. At around 3 a.m. I was approached by two young boys, who must have been no more than twelve years old. They strolled over to me, sat down on the kerb next to me and started to chat. 'Did you chase that stolen car last weekend?' one of them asked me. I had no idea what he was talking about. 'It got burnt out over the park,' he proudly told me.

The lads went on to mention the names of various people that they clearly thought I'd recognise, unaware of the fact I was only working my first shift as a police officer. After about ten minutes it dawned on me: it's 3 a.m. and these are young boys. It was like a different world, literally, yet at the time I lived just a few miles away.

After a while they walked off into the night. Their world was very different to mine and that of the majority of people. They were out in the middle of the night and it didn't appear that anyone had missed them. Maybe they just didn't care. Over the next eighteen years, I was going to find out just how different lives can be.

I only managed a couple of shifts as a volunteer as, surprisingly, I was accepted on to the regular force and soon started my training as a full-time officer. I had to endure fifteen weeks at the Police Training College in Ashford in Kent. I say endure and I mean it! It was a strange few months, with lots of revising and studying but also lots of new challenges. Living in a hotel for that length of time, being in a classroom every day and having to get to know lots and lots of new people was exhausting, and every day we were being exposed to a new experience or yet another role play. It was a great way to learn and it definitely introduced me to the pressure you feel in the job, but I don't think anyone would say they enjoyed their time there.

It also involved getting used to being a police officer and to the effect that would have on our daily lives – where you go, who you socialise with, where you live; for some more than others, that would mean pretty big changes. I studied really hard at training college and was privileged to be awarded the Baton of Honour at the passing-out parade. It was given to the top-performing student from the intake of around a hundred and fifty officers. It was an incredibly proud moment both for me and for Suffolk Police, as it recognised the effort that had been put in over the four months of training.

And so, I was up and running. I was a real cop about to hit the mean streets of Suffolk!

3

This guy has got potential

NOVEMBER 2001. I remember it like it was yesterday. I may not have enjoyed training school – it was all very intense and took me completely out of my comfort zone – but suddenly here I was: first day, brand new, out of the box. A fully fledged police officer. When I joined the police, I was asked to nominate where I'd like to be based. You got three choices, so I started with Ipswich and then picked the two areas just outside it, as they would be easy to get to and busy enough places to learn the job without jumping straight in the deep end. To be fair, I should have realised that meant I'd be stationed some 30 miles away in a place I'd barely heard of and most definitely never visited. Welcome to the police!

As I'm sure most people would, I decided to take a drive out there before I started, just to see the lie of the land and familiarise myself with the town. It was a little place called Leiston. I recall driving through it, frantically looking around and distinctly questioning if this could actually be it. It seemed a tiny place, so why on earth did it need a police station at all? Little did I know that, in fact, we'd be covering almost 100 square miles, so the town would be just a small part of my work. I was about to be introduced to rural policing. Leiston is an interesting town situated in coastal Suffolk, which is a beautiful part of the world. It had clearly grown a lot and there was now a fair amount of unemployment, deprivation and drugs, so, suffice to say, there was a reasonable amount of crime as well.

When I met the team on my first day, they seemed really nice and certainly made me feel very welcome. The team was a mix of some young-in-service, proactive, almost excitable cops and some who had definitely been there, seen it and done it. Looking back, that was probably the secret to our success as a team, as everyone knew their role and each brought something slightly different to the party.

One of the most significant moments of that first day was meeting my tutor constable. His job was to show me the ropes and help me put into practice what I'd been taught at training school. He was a massive influence on me as a police officer. As any fresh-faced recruit will soon discover, your tutor constable introduces you to a whole new world, and their approach will undoubtedly rub off on you. That's hardly surprising – you are embarking on a career that is fraught with danger, incredibly demanding and full of experiences you are very unlikely to have encountered before. Your tutor is there to keep you safe and on the right track, and to keep the unsuspecting public safe too. You need the tutor more than they need you, so you listen to every word they say and watch everything they do.

My tutor was PC Jamie Hollis. Predictably, he was affectionately known as Reg, but unlike his namesake from Sunhill on TV's *The Bill*, he was a fiery, lively, headstrong individual. He was also incredibly kind and caring, a genuinely nice guy, but he would take no prisoners! He told me very early on that his view was that the police are not there to make honest, hard-working people's lives difficult, as life can be difficult enough, so he expected me to show discretion and judgement. 'We are here to make the lives of criminals uncomfortable,' he said. I remember thinking that this summed up policing in many respects; people who are in need or who are vulnerable should be handled with kid gloves and kindness, but those who are violent, aggressive and intent on committing crime should be handled in a completely different way. Jamie struck that balance and I remember thinking I'd try and take that with me. He also told me over and over again that I'd have to be willing to make decisions and stand by them. Policing is not for the faint hearted and if you're not prepared to make decisions then you're in the wrong job. He was spot on; it's a tough job in which you are sometimes damned if you do and damned if you don't. And, rest assured, whatever decision you make it's unlikely that you'll keep everyone happy.

On the first shift, as we gradually got to know each other, we drove around a bit and stopped a few cars. My job over the ten-week tutor period was to observe for the first few weeks during such patrols, after which I gradually started to take the lead with the aim of achieving independent patrol by the end.

It was a strange sensation being out and about in a marked police car. It is the closest I think you can get to being in a goldfish bowl: everyone looking in at you and you looking out at them. And I was nervous, really nervous. I'd pretty much come straight from school, having dropped out of university, and suddenly this wasn't training any more; it wasn't a role play, hypothetical question or a discussion in class. This was real life, real people and real risk.

I'd lived a very sheltered life in many respects. I'd gone to a good school, had lots of good friends and, through sport, had travelled the world and met lots of good people. Now I was going to put myself in harm's way and deal with some of the most dangerous people in society.

It got to about 10 p.m. and I'd almost finished my first shift as a police officer. It had all gone pretty well really. I'd met the team, I'd got all my kit sorted out and I had started to get to know Jamie. We certainly hadn't come across anything that caused me any great concern and I remember thinking, *This is OK, I can do this!*

As we were just about to arrive back at the station, the radio crackled into life and part of a transmission came through about a domestic incident taking place. I'd no idea where this particular village was; perhaps it was covered by someone else, I thought, and we wouldn't need to worry about it? Jamie turned, looked at me, and with a glint in his eye and a cheeky smile said, 'We'll go to that!' He flicked some switches on the dashboard and we were off.

If you've never been driven in a police car during a blue-light run, then it's hard to describe just what it's like. I certainly wouldn't call it comfortable – there is a lot of accelerating, braking and overtaking, and despite what any police driver tells you, it's not smooth. Lots of people think the police have specially mapped cars with high-performance engines and sports suspension. No, not when you're on a response team in rural Suffolk. We were driving a diesel Ford Escort, which sounded like a bag of nails, probably because it had been driven flat out several times too often.

We set off at a rate of knots, blue light bouncing off trees and hedges as we left the sanctuary of the town and plunged into the darkness of the countryside beyond. Jamie warned me, 'This guy has got potential, so just be careful.'

I appreciated the warning, but it filled me with even more adrenaline, if that were possible. What did that mean exactly: 'He's got potential'? I took it to mean he could be a tricky person to deal with. I also made the assumption that Jamie had dealt with this guy before.

It seemed to take us moments to arrive, but in fact we'd travelled at least ten miles. I'd spent the journey eagerly, nervously, anticipating what we'd find when we arrived, my mind a bit of a blur. As we got to the address, I remember thinking that I'd just follow Jamie's lead. Fortunately, another officer had arrived as well, so between them they would deal with it and I'd just be along for the ride.

The road was dark, with only the occasional streetlight offering any illumination, and it was eerily quiet. Jamie confidently strode up to the door of the house, which was promptly opened by a man inside. He was diminutive, with short-cropped hair, but he had that look; a look that made me nervous. Not the sort of person I'd want to meet down a dark alley on my own. Perhaps that's what Jamie had meant when he said to be careful.

The guy went back inside and Jamie followed behind, with me tailing afterwards. It was a curious introduction: no conversation on the doorstep or the man asking what we were doing there; just an acceptance that we had arrived and then in we went. Once we were inside, a woman made herself known to us; she was drunk and obnoxious, her every other word being an obscenity. I stood back, surveying the cluttered front room, watching my two experienced colleagues trying to find out what had happened and calm the situation down.

While driving to the incident we'd been told on the radio that there was a long history of drink-fuelled domestics involving this couple, and tonight seemed to be no different. Both of them were highly intoxicated and, much to my amazement, there was a young baby in the house, no more than a few months old. The woman was holding the child and the discussions between all parties seemed amicable, notwithstanding the colourful language and clear animosity for the police. It's important to say, I did not have a clue what was going on at this stage! Powers, policies, procedures, they all seemed a bit muddled to me at that time, and all I kept thinking about was Jamie saying 'Be careful.' Had I been asked to sort this out by myself, I think I'd have had a complete meltdown – this didn't feel like any of the role plays we'd done before.

Although on edge, I was relieved that the guy seemed essentially meek and mild; stood at the back of the living room, not really saying much and certainly not threatening any violence. Perhaps he was a changed man. I remember the woman passing the baby to him as she became a little more animated and upset, which reassured me still further that this was not going to escalate now – how could it with a newborn in the house?

After a bit more negotiation, Jamie made the decision. The woman was going to have to be arrested to prevent a breach of the peace. It's an expression that is used a lot, and it basically refers to a situation when harm – meaning violence – is done or is likely to be done. Jamie was clearly not happy with leaving both parties in the house, and as the man was calm and compliant it was the woman who would be spending the night sobering up in the cells. It seemed to make sense to me; at least we wouldn't need to arrest him, which would be a right result.

As the words were said and the woman was told she was being arrested, all hell broke loose. She stood up and began to swing her arms wildly. 'Fuck off, leave me alone!' she screamed in my colleagues' faces. Jamie and the other officer ducked to avoid being hit by a flailing hand, and then frantically struggled to restrain her, but she threw herself to the floor, screaming and yelling. All of a sudden, it was as though a switch had been flicked and the man had been ignited with fury.

'Get your fucking hands off her!' he shouted. He dropped the baby on the floor and flew across the living room at Jamie. I was stunned, shocked, speechless. More pertinently, I was smack-bang in the way. I was pushed back down the hallway as we all retreated out of the front door as fast as we possibly could.

The man was now the character Jamie had spoken about. The 'potential' that cops refer to – this guy had it in spades.

His eyes were wide and wild as he stood in a fighting stance, guarding the front door of the house with fists clenched and shouting threats. 'Come on, then, you think you're a fucking big man!' He stood there slightly elevated on the doorstep, reminiscent of a boxer standing in his corner at the start of a bout, itching to cross the ring to confront his opponent.

Jamie racked his baton and the other officer drew her CS spray. 'Get back!' shouted Jamie. I was stood some metres further away, absolutely motionless in the middle of the front garden in the near pitch black; I might as well have been a statue.

You often hear people talk of the fight-or-flight response we have when encountering dangerous situations. There is another element to that; it's 'freeze', and that's what I'd done: completely frozen. It was as though I wasn't actually there any more. As a nineteen-year-old lad who had never been in a fight in my life, I was suddenly having to deal with violent criminals who clearly had no respect for the uniform or the law, and who had no qualms about attacking a police officer. I knew from past reports that this guy had assaulted his partner many times; presumably he thought that was OK. But for the police to lay hands on her to arrest her, that was not OK. Illogical? Yes, of course, but he didn't strike me as a logical type any more. It resonated with me that we were there trying to make sure everyone was safe, yet the people now at the highest risk of being harmed were us. It was something I'd get used to over the years.

The stand-off continued for what seemed like an eternity before some additional officers arrived and things started to calm down a bit. The man lowered his tone and dropped his hands down by his sides, fists no longer clenched and ready for battle. He seemed far calmer now that we were all outside and making no attempt to get back in. One of the officers who arrived knew the guy well and, much to my amazement, strolled over to him with his hands in his pockets and a cheeky, 'All right, mate, what's the matter? What's happened?' Before we knew it, the man was having a roll-up with the officer, and his girlfriend had done a miraculous job of sobering up; all seemed calm again.

After much deliberation Jamie and the other officers on the team managed to broker a deal that involved nobody being arrested but the parties staying at different addresses overnight. As I say, I had little understanding of what was happening, let alone why the decision was being made; I was just glad to be leaving in one piece. Much to our surprise, and great relief, the baby was absolutely fine too; completely oblivious of the drama that had unfolded in front of them.

As we drove back to the station, we had a chat about the incident. Jamie seemed pretty unfazed by it all, as though it was business as usual and nothing out of the ordinary. I remember him saying, 'You've got to keep your wits about you, as these things have a habit of escalating.' And I also remember thinking, *I'm not really sure I want to spend my working life with my wits about me, waiting for the next violent outburst.* The shift finished and I drove home in a bit of a daze.

I'd left university after a matter of weeks because I wanted to join the police. I'd then spent months in training, but now, on my first day, here I was questioning if it was the job for me. I kept going over the incident in my mind, thinking about what could have happened and reflecting on my complete inaction. It's fair to say, I didn't sleep well.

The following day I met my dear old ma for a coffee in town. We sat right at the back of the shop, speaking in hushed tones so that other people couldn't overhear our conversation, and I regaled her with the events of the night before. 'I couldn't believe it: he just dropped the baby and flew at Jamie.' My mum didn't really say a lot. She was probably as perplexed as I was.

As you'd expect, my parents were very proud of me becoming a police officer and they would have spent the previous evening nervously waiting to hear how it went. This wouldn't necessarily have been what they expected. I was unloading it all, looking for reassurance; perhaps looking for a way out; maybe even hoping that we could agree this wasn't the job for me after all. I couldn't understand why police officers would go to work every day to be attacked and threatened in the way we had been the night before. Surely that's not what we get paid for?

I decided to see how things went and to stick with it for the time being, but I fully expected I'd be leaving the force barely after I'd started.

Little did I know that as the months and years passed, such incidents would become those I particularly wanted to be involved in; most coppers are the same. No longer would I be the rookie rooted to the spot wishing I could be anywhere else but there. As we grow more experienced, the bullies don't seem that bad any more; there's always someone bigger, stronger, angrier and more violent, so the chances are things are never quite as bad as they could be.

As a police officer you take great pride in standing up to the people who threaten others. I often think of a line from a poem by Michael Mark*:

> And maybe just remind the few, if ill of us they speak,
> that we are all that stands between
> the monsters and the weak.

I remember the first occasion I read that poem – by which point I'd been in the police for some time – and thinking how absolutely true it was. There is often a lot of criticism of the police, yet not many people would want to be living in a society without them. I've even had several criminals tell me how grim a world it would be without the police. Not many want to confront violent and potentially dangerous individuals; they leave that to us.

* Excerpt from the poem *Monsters and the Weak* by Michael Marks, 2006

4

Cheryl

IPSWICH, 18 JUNE 2005. I had been a police officer for four years and was now a sergeant. My night shift wasn't due to start until 11 p.m., so I was sitting in a restaurant having dinner with my family when I got a call from a private number. That normally means it's work and that something significant has happened. This was no different, but it was the worst call I've ever taken.

'There's been a polac,' said the caller. This is the term used for an accident involving a police vehicle; they happen all the time, which is not surprising given the number of incidents the police respond to. In the vast majority of cases they are relatively minor and very rarely are people seriously injured. 'It's a fatal.' I could not believe what I was hearing. I hesitated, silently trying to take that in.

I remember asking, 'The fatality, is it police or public?' The answer seemed to take an age to come back, but come back it did.

'Police. Cheryl has died and it looks like Chris won't make it.' I was stunned, rocked to the core. I knew them both very well; they were good friends. As our teams overlapped on shifts,

I'd seen them almost every day, and I'd attended hundreds and hundreds of calls with them over the years.

Cheryl was someone who everyone knew at the nick; friendly, hardworking and never far from the action. I quickly finished the call, told my family that I had to go, and within what seemed like a minute I was walking into the police station at Civic Drive still in a complete state of shock.

I had no idea what to expect when I walked in, but now, more than ever, we needed to come together. As soon as I arrived, I started ringing round officers on our team, and every one of them dropped everything and made their way to work. We would be tasked with covering 'normal policing' and taking over from the team on duty. It was a horrible situation to be in – having to carry on the emergency work that is a core function of our job, yet against the most tragic, devastating backdrop of what had happened.

I was very conscious that most of the team on duty had not yet been told what had happened. They knew there had been a serious accident and they knew that their teammates were badly hurt; they still didn't know just how bad it was.

I called and spoke to the two sergeants from Cheryl's team, Matt and Rocky, who had already been informed. They were fantastic sergeants and their team was like a family. I remember admiring the work ethic and team spirit they had and hoping that our team would be viewed in a similar way. They looked out for each other and nobody was ever left behind. The conversation started very tentatively. 'I just don't know what to say; I just can't believe it still,' I said.

They both sounded numb as we talked, almost as though they were running on autopilot. *How on earth will they cope with this?* I thought.

'We need to get the team together to tell them,' Matt said quietly.

As my own team started to arrive, I told them the scantest details and out they went, while gradually Cheryl's team began arriving at the station. They all went upstairs to the conference room on the third floor, and I suspect the more worldly wise among them would have already been fearing the worst. I desperately tried to avoid them, as I was dreading them asking me what I knew. I'd never have broken the confidence of Matt and Rocky, but it would have been written all over my face.

The sergeants' office in the old Ipswich nick was a small room on the ground floor, and it was generally the centre of activity. The vast majority of the time the door was open and there'd be a constant flow of officers in and out, asking various questions and getting paperwork signed. It was also a fun place; you'd often hear raucous laughter and relentless piss taking. Not that night. That door barely opened, so I sat in there on my own, desperately trying to come to terms with what had happened and working out how we would keep the nick afloat.

After a while the door opened and in walked Rocky and Matt. 'Do you want me to tell them?' I asked. They didn't; this was their team and they wanted to do it; I respected them hugely for that. I told them that I couldn't think of two better sergeants to look after their colleagues in such traumatic circumstances. 'Your team need you more now than ever, but you also need each other.'

We went upstairs to the canteen and they continued into the conference room. They seemed to be in there no time at all, but the reality was that time had lost its meaning for all of us. I popped to the gents and, just as I was about to leave, in walked

Matt. He broke down, completely distraught. He'd just had to tell his team that their dear friend Cheryl had died and that Chris was being rushed to Addenbrooke's – a large hospital in Cambridge, which was the nearest facility offering the intensive, specialist care he needed. What prepares you for that? Nothing does. I put my arm round Matt's shoulder and hugged him. I had nothing to say; there *was* nothing to say. Strong and silent was all I could be for him.

Within moments, though, Matt regained his composure; his number-one priority was the team, and with steely determination and resilience he was going to be there for them. He and Rocky had to lead their team through the darkest of days. He had to start calling the officers on the team who were on leave, and then go to the hospital.

The rest of his team stayed in the conference room for a long time, and to this day I don't know what was said; it's none of my business. They had to try to take in what had happened and they needed time to do that.

Initially, I knew very little of what had happened, but gradually things became clearer. Cheryl and Chris had been responding to an urgent call, driving with blue lights on – something they would have done thousands of times before. As Cheryl negotiated a sweeping right-hand bend, she lost control of the car and it slammed into the back of a parked lorry.

I returned to my duties that night, but everything was completely eclipsed by the trauma and desolation of a friend losing her life doing the job she loved and was very good at.

A little later in the shift, one of our team returned from the hospital. He had been sent there to act as the Coroner's Officer. It's a role that police officers carry out alarmingly regularly, sometimes daily. It involves completing paperwork and acting on behalf of the Coroner. It's all about establishing the facts of how someone has suddenly died. I'd asked one of my most experienced, most robust officers to do it for Cheryl. It would, I hoped, be the one and only time he'd ever be the Coroner's Officer for a friend and colleague.

He returned to the police station with a bag of belongings, and as he walked into the sergeants' office, he looked utterly exhausted and emotionally spent. He placed the bag down on the desk, and I began to look through the contents. The first two items were Cheryl's stab-proof vest and her notebook. Both were now drenched in blood. It stopped me in my tracks; a moment I will never forget and one that still almost brings me to tears when I allow myself to think about it.

It was the toughest of nights; I had colleagues questioning why they do the job, why they continue putting their lives at risk in the name of public duty – some even contemplating their own mortality. It's testament to their character that they remained professional throughout.

As the evening turned to night, our team met at the police station. I was very conscious that we would all have been hugely affected by what had happened, and that we – like Matt and Rocky's team – needed time to come to terms with it. We were all friends of Cheryl and Chris too. We agreed to meet at the scene of the accident that night at 4 a.m.; it seemed like the only place to go and pay our respects.

Throughout my years as a police officer I had seen countless friends and family attend scenes where their loved ones had died; sometimes car accidents, sometimes murders. I remember, particularly, being on the scene of the Soham murders. I was only twenty years old and had barely been in the police for a year. It was an experience that would stay with me for a long time. I was there when the parents of Holly Wells and Jessica Chapman came to see where their beloved daughters had been found. As a young officer, it was incredibly traumatic, yet I was blown away by their dignity and poise.

As Kevin Wells, Holly's father, walked down the muddy track towards where I was standing, I froze to the spot. Should I say something? Should I look the other way? Perhaps I should offer my condolences? Before I had a chance to decide, he gave me a warm smile and said, 'Thanks for everything you're doing, we really appreciate it.' I was speechless.

The whole experience of the Soham murders shook me to the core. I recall another moment that occurred the day afterwards. I was stood near the main road, and a young boy – no more than six or seven years old – came walking down the verge hand in hand with his father. As he got closer I could see that he was holding a teddy bear tightly against his chest and his dad was holding some flowers. The young boy gave me the teddy bear and asked, 'Can you put it with all the flowers, please?' With the teddy was a card with a message addressed to Holly and Jessica.

I had tears in my eyes and found it hard to speak. 'Of course, thank you.' It was the least I could do. As the boy began to walk away in the drizzling rain, the enormity of what had happened truly hit me.

Now that Cheryl had died, we were going to visit the scene, and we knew it would be so, so tough. As the time drew nearer, I was absolutely dreading it. West End Road is a long straight road on the outskirts of Ipswich town centre. I arrived at the scene with the other sergeant on our team and we parked up a few minutes before other people arrived. It felt surreal, almost beyond belief, that a few hours earlier the scene had been so different; now, other than the yellow paint marks on the road – laid down to mark out the details of the accident – it was back to how it had always been.

All of a sudden the entire team arrived; it was as though they had been waiting round the corner until it was 4 a.m. on the dot. We all got out of our vehicles and just stood in disbelief. There was not a lot of talking; some officers walked up and down staring blankly into space, some stood silently with each other, and some just couldn't face it and had to leave.

Policing can sometimes feel a little bit removed from reality, which is ironic given that it's the harsh realities of life that we deal with. I often reflected on that when dealing with tragedy; I was empathetic and could feel the raw emotion, but it was not me personally who had lost a friend or family member. This was suddenly different; Cheryl was our friend and she had been doing the job we all do. Reality was slowly sinking in. Many colleagues had bought flowers and they began laying them at the scene, whispering a prayer as they did so. The sun was just starting to come up, heralding a beautiful summer's day, which I thought was very fitting for someone like Cheryl. Although our thoughts were chiefly with her in those moments, we were also, of course, praying that Chris would pull through.

News of the accident broke the next day and it cast a shadow over the whole town. People will have their views on the police and they may be quite critical at times, but when tragedy strikes it shows that the vast majority of the public really care about them. They appreciate the risks that the police take and often comment that there's no way they could do the job themselves. In the shifts that followed, I lost count of how many criminals came and spoke to me, to offer their condolences. Some of it was pretty blunt – 'Oi, Livingstone, I'm sorry about the copper that died' – while others were as eloquent as they were sincere, and for that I was incredibly appreciative. Don't get me wrong, some were not sympathetic at all, instead immaturely taking some abhorrent pleasure in what had happened. What can I say other than 'Shame on them'?

As the days moved on, we began to prepare for the funeral. I had never been to a funeral of the size and magnitude of this, and while it was desperately sad, it was also incredibly humbling and inspiring, hearing about the life and work of Cheryl.

Her team formed a guard of honour and were also the pall-bearers; the streets outside the church were lined with officers in uniform, all there to pay their respects and, importantly, to support Cheryl's family and team. It was something that I will never ever forget.

I have remained good friends with Matt and Rocky, and I have the utmost respect for them and the way they supported Cheryl's family and the team while dealing with their own grief; I am in awe of their strength and compassion. Sue, Cheryl's sister, has become a prominent campaigner and advocate for the COPS (Care of Police Survivors) charity that supports police survivors. I often follow the work she does and it reminds me of just how utterly tragic the events of that evening were for her family.

I had always known that policing was dangerous and that, very occasionally, police officers lose their lives in the line of duty, but this was the biggest reality check anyone could ever have. It was a responsibility that I had always taken very seriously, to ensure that everyone got home safely, but from that day forth it took on a whole new poignancy. Every year, on 18 June, I remember two things: the day I joined the police, and the day that a friend lost her life doing that very same job.

5

Serial killer in our town

IPSWICH, LIKE ALMOST every other town of its size in the UK, had an issue with prostitution and an active red-light district. It was something that people knew went on and that the police, normally through the local beat officers, would try to disrupt and deal with. That was all about to change in 2006 when Ipswich was thrust into the spotlight for all the wrong reasons. It was about to come under the glare of the world's media when a young sex worker went missing and then a body was found.

I was a police officer in Ipswich at the time and the investigation initially started as a missing person enquiry. Missing person reports are very common and often relate to young people or those who have lived a more chaotic lifestyle. I guess this incident was no different initially, but then concern began to grow, and when the first body was found it became a murder investigation.

All policing operations are given a randomly selected name, one that's typically soon forgotten once the operation is finished. Not this time. Operation Sumac was going to become a once-in-a-career policing event for us all, and its effects would be felt for many, many years after.

The next few months became a high-profile investigation into a serial killer. I remember being sat at Ipswich Police Station, waiting for a highly anticipated press conference to be broadcast live from Headquarters. The TV room gradually filled with officers from all ranks, including the Chief Superintendent responsible for policing in the south of Suffolk. The press conference began and we were all confident there must be a significant update coming; we knew in our hearts that another body had been found.

The Senior Investigating Officer, Stewart Gull, began the press conference and confirmed that a body had indeed been found. What he then went on to say stunned the room. While examining the scene of the first discovery, they had found a second body close by. You could have heard a pin drop. Experienced, seasoned officers who had been there and done it all before were transfixed by the screen, hanging on every word that was being said. Despite my suspicions, I still could not believe it. This meant there was now a serial killer somewhere in our town, taking vulnerable women off the streets and murdering them in cold blood. As the broadcast came to an end, the room just sat silently for a moment and then gradually began to crackle into life.

It was testament to the investigation team and senior leadership that nobody had known the news until it broke. The situation had to be carefully managed, because as the press descended on the town they all wanted to know what was going on. This shit had just got real.

The effect that the murders had was nuclear. Ipswich is a busy place and most definitely the centre of crime and policing activity in the county, but Suffolk's police is predominantly a rural force with very limited resources in comparison; that was until Op Sumac got into full swing. With every discovery of a body – there would be five victims in total – came another huge resourcing implication: officers to guard the crime scenes 24/7, search teams, crime scene investigators, detectives to follow up on lines of enquiry, and thousands and thousands of hours of CCTV to be reviewed. One murder scene is a challenge, but when you have multiple scenes in large rural locations it becomes incredibly difficult.

To preserve a crime scene within a house is pretty simple; just a handful of officers needed, and the forensic examination won't take long. Transfer that into a large open area and the numbers go up, and up again. Not to mention that it was happening at the harshest time of year when the temperature seemed permanently stuck below zero. And all the time normal business carries on; the majority of the things that were important before remain so, and the public still expect to receive a response when they need it.

As a local officer, I found it surreal to see the hundreds of officers being drafted in to the county. I remember a conversation with a senior officer from Merseyside. They had come down to Ipswich with a fleet of high-powered police cars kitted out with the latest in Automatic Number Plate Recognition technology.

The support the public gave us was amazing; everywhere we went we were greeted with kindness and encouragement. I remember on Christmas Day I was parked near to a roundabout in town and a little old lady appeared, knocked on the window and gave me a paper plate filled with sausage rolls and a piece of cake. That never normally happens, but it showed just how united the town had become in the face of adversity.

As well as dealing with 'normal business', we all wanted to do our bit. I remember, as the operation rumbled on, starting a night shift and, despite the fatigue written all over people's faces, everyone was in early – really early – and all of them wanting to get out there. I took the murders very personally, not because it was my investigation to solve, but because it was my town: the town I was born in, that I grew up in and that was my home.

The crimes were cold and callous, and all of the victims were known to me. Tania Nicol, Gemma Adams, Anneli Alderton, Paula Clennell and Annette Nicholls. I'd spoken to them all on many occasions. Nobody deserves to have their life taken from them, and these women were no different. It seemed that every spare minute of our shift was spent patrolling the red-light district, stopping cars, speaking to members of the public; all of us desperately seeking that nugget of information.

There was much speculation about who could commit such offences and the inevitable queue of experts were wheeled out to give their opinion. Amazingly, all the time that the murders were taking place, we still had young women working the streets. It seemed unfathomable that they would take such risks and it showed just how their addictions had gripped their lives. A lot of our time was spent in and around the areas where the women had been known to frequent to try and stop any more murders.

I remember the night that Steve Wright was arrested like it was yesterday. I was on a night shift (we seemed to work a lot of night shifts at that time!) and at around 5 a.m. I got a call from a colleague to tell me that an arrest had just been made. 'What do you mean it's been made? How has that happened and none of us knew about it?' But I already knew what was about to happen: I was going to be asked to find a stack of officers to assist with scene management and chaos was about to ensue.

I arrived at London Road and I was briefed on what my colleagues needed and I then had to make it happen. We all anticipated that the news would break very quickly, particularly as the arrest had been made in the heart of the red-light district, so we didn't have long. We would need to ensure the house was secure but also manage the surrounding area and that wasn't going to be easy. Police scenes are normally pretty dull places for officers – the blue-and-white cordon tape is placed across roads, pavements and gardens, and it never ceased to amaze me how such a flimsy bit of plastic stops people in their tracks. Perhaps not on this occasion, though: the temptation of seeing what was going on would be too much for some.

London Road is a busy place with lots of houses and lots of footfall. The cordons were put in place and gradually, as the sun rose, so too did the activity levels. I had cops on every corner and all of them seemed to be surrounded by gaggles of people wanting to know what was happening. Had there been another murder? Had we found another body? We had been at work for around twelve hours already but nobody was feeling particularly fatigued or tired; this was what we had all been waiting for.

I was given the near impossible task of trying to prevent the media getting too close. Not sure how I was going to do that, but I could ensure that they didn't enter the scene. After an hour or two, I was made aware that there seemed to be a news crew in the B & B on the other side of the road and they were peering through the net curtains directly opposite the house.

I went and spoke to the owner, and asked if I could speak to the news crew. There seemed to be some confusion because the owner gave the impression that there was nobody inside. I went up the stairs and into the room to find a slightly embarrassed reporter standing behind the door, trying to look inconspicuous! We had no legal powers to prevent this reporter and their colleagues from covering the arrest and, of course, it was important that it was reported; the media are our greatest help with so many investigations but I just wanted to make sure they understood just how important it was that nothing was broadcast or put out there that could jeopardise the case. They were local reporters and they were fantastic throughout; something some of their national and international colleagues could have done with copying.

Police Headquarters was now being guarded by special constables; not an easy task as journalists tried to sneak through doors, pretending to be members of staff and even setting up long-range microphones to capture what officers were saying as they walked to their cars. I remember encountering one shady character at the threshold of the building but before I had a chance to ask any questions he was gone. It felt like we were under siege.

Once Steve Wright had been arrested everyone wanted to know more about him. He was certainly not someone that I had heard of before but gradually more and more details became known. His Ford Mondeo was a car that some officers were familiar with, having seen it in and around the area, and some had even stopped him in it. And it also became clear that the case was going to hinge on forensic evidence and, to that end, no stone would be left unturned. His car was taken away on a trailer, wrapped in a protective cover to ensure that no evidence would be lost, and the detailed, painstaking forensic examination of his house would go on for days and days and days.

The arrest led to charges and the charges led to one of the most high-profile criminal trials in living memory. Suddenly Ipswich Crown Court seemed to become the centre for the world's media. Satellite trucks filled every car park and journalists tried to jostle for the best vantage points so that they could get just the right backdrop for their live reports.

The trial started in dramatic fashion with the first jury being discharged after one of the jurors fell ill but proceedings got underway on 14 January 2008. It would grip not only Ipswich but the whole country. We all knew that the trial would take many, many weeks but as we neared the end the anticipation grew and grew. None of us already knew the evidence as it was tightly controlled by the Major Investigation Team so we were hearing it for the first time as well.

And then came the judgment on 21 February: guilty of all five murders. The very next day Wright was sentenced to a whole-life term – he'd never see the light of day as a free man again. For many people within the community this was what they wanted and they felt that it brought the whole episode to an end. For the police and the local authorities, it most certainly didn't. We needed to make sure that this never happened again.

In the aftermath of the murders, but long before the trial had even reached court, the police and partners set the objective of removing prostitution from the streets of Ipswich within five years. I was honoured to be asked to help with the tactical part of the operation and I was tasked to come up with a plan. I thought back to how, even while they knew there was a serial killer in our midst, the sex workers kept working. That showed us all within the team that this would be a difficult nut to crack. We agreed that, first, we would try to remove the demand, and that would be my job.

I knew the red-light area of Ipswich really well as it was a stone's throw from the police station, but in truth it was not somewhere that I'd ever been other than in a marked police car. I also didn't know a great deal about the kind of men who used prostitutes; were they young, old, known to the police? I had no idea.

I wrote the operational order and we set about our work. I was stunned by the results. The red-light area was like the North Circular at times, with a steady stream of kerb crawlers trawling the streets. They would be seen time and time again, driving round and round.

The women would often work in particular areas and would wave at the cars as they went past. Our tactics were simple: wait for the women to be picked up and then, once we knew roughly where they were going, we'd move in.

It was like shooting fish in a barrel as these were not hardened, streetwise criminals: these were men who were invariably not known to the police and had no idea about how we worked. Most shifts started just after dark and we'd track the movement of the women on CCTV cameras. Some nights we'd arrest three or four men, all of whom had come to Ipswich looking to pay for sex and then ended their night locked in a police cell with the enormity of what had happened slowly sinking in.

We had agreed very early on that the women would not be prosecuted in those early days as it was likely to be counterproductive. They'd go to court, probably get fined, and then have to work even harder to fund their addiction and pay their fines. We needed to help them out of addiction and into a less chaotic lifestyle.

As the weeks went on the arrests for kerb crawling just kept coming in. At this point, we had to decide how best to deal with them as we wanted to ensure that they never came to our attention again. Some other forces had run courses for first-time offenders but the sense I was getting was that these men had been given the fright of their life and the vast majority would never run the risk of being caught again. The statistics were also backing that up; we arrested and cautioned over a hundred and fifty men and only one or two reoffended. They were taken to court and we were successful in obtaining Anti-Social Behaviour Orders. These were men who were out of their depth with the police and, all of a sudden, they had an ASBO to their name and they were being named and shamed by the press.

We also became aware of just how many cars are registered in the wife's name and not the husband's! That got a little awkward as we'd record the registrations of vehicles seen several times in and around the red-light district irrespective of whether they were spoken to or not.

I was asked to compose the letter that would be sent to the registered owners and, as I wrote it, I could only imagine how uncomfortable that conversation would be as we listed the times and locations the vehicles had been seen driving in the area.

'I am writing to inform you that your vehicle was seen by police in an area known to be frequented by sex workers.' I was sure that would get their attention. *'Your vehicle was seen on eight occasions, including in areas that are for access only.'* Ouch!

Depending on what had been seen we'd often add a bit more information so that there could be no misunderstandings. *'The driver of the vehicle was seen stopping and speaking to lone females within the red-light area.'* Hopefully they had a satisfactory explanation, not for us because we weren't asking, but I know who might have been!

Over the months that followed, the area changed beyond all recognition. No longer was it being used by hundreds of cars and the quiet residential streets became exactly that. The number of women being seen working also reduced and the feedback from our vice officers was that they were engaging really well; the multi-agency team were able to help them with housing, healthcare, dentistry and, most importantly, their addictions, all throughout the time that we were hammering the kerb crawlers night after night.

The two parts of the operation were working in tandem and having some great results. It is testament to the team that nobody ever lost sight of the fact that this was to change the lives of so many people for the better.

I would estimate that at one point we had up to fifty women known to be working the streets, but as time went on, we were left with a handful who were failing to engage and, despite the police activity, they continued to flout the law. I remember the meeting where we discussed the issue and agreed that after almost a year of engagement and support, it was now time to flex a bit of muscle.

We went out on patrol as usual in unmarked cars and a short time later one of our most prolific sex workers appeared and was picked up by a man in a car. We arrived on the scene a few moments later and found her and her client in a state of undress, in the back of the car in a quiet residential car park. I opened the car door. 'Do you want to get yourself dressed, fella?' The man frantically began grabbing for his trousers, which were around his ankles.

The female jumped out of the car, hurriedly getting dressed. 'I want my money, Livingstone; I'm not going until I've been paid.'

I told her she wasn't getting paid, she was getting nicked. She knew me well as we'd encountered her over thirty times in similar situations over the last twelve months.

'No, Livingstone, we don't get arrested.'

I said to her, 'That was last week, this week you get locked up.'

As my colleague began to apply the handcuffs, she shouted back, 'You're such a prick, Livingstone, I fucking hate you.' Both her and the guy were taken to the cells and the woman was remanded in custody and taken to court the following day. She was issued with an ASBO. Over the next few weeks the last remaining women were targeted and put before the courts.

I remember visiting King's Cross in London and speaking to the local vice team, and they explained some of the issues that they had encountered. They gave the example of three sex workers who were all due to be taken to court and ASBOs applied for. None of them made it as they all died while working as prostitutes. One was murdered and found floating in the Thames, one got into a dispute with a punter who drove off in his lorry and ran her over, and the other one fell from a balcony while high on drugs. If that isn't the most compelling of submissions put before a court then I don't know what is; not to mention the unbearable effect it was having on the local community. Needles and used condoms in car parks and the front gardens of houses were a common sight before we started the operation, but not any more.

This was the very best example I was involved in of tackling a problem and being successful. It was never going to be achieved through enforcement alone, as the demand would still be there for both the workers and the punters. It required buy-in from the community, from the police and, most importantly, from partner organisations.

I still often think back to Op Sumac and the women who lost their lives. It will for ever be a black mark in the history of Ipswich, but the response was something that fills me with pride.

6

Sorry, who is getting demoted?

I'VE HAD A slightly odd career. When I first joined the police I was, like so many recruits, really ambitious and determined to progress up the organisation. To that end, when I was in my first year, I applied for the accelerated promotion scheme as that would enable me to move up the ranks quickly. I wasn't successful and, in all honesty, I was not surprised: what they were looking for was simply beyond me as a new recruit who had come straight from school.

I did decide, though, that I would take my sergeant's exam and see if I could get through that at the end of my two-year probationary period. The good news was that this was the first year that they had elected to hold an additional sitting of the exam; the bad news was that they announced it late and I only had six weeks to revise for it.

People who know me will say that I can be a little obsessive and this was no different – I revised every day, every weekend, hours and hours a day, and even while I was sitting in the back of a police car while working on the drugs team. It took over my life as I had decided it was what I wanted to do and it was important. I firmly believe that if something is important in life you should do it at full throttle.

I took the exam and passed it with a decent score. I come from a family that is really supportive and encouraging but if I came home and told my father that I had got 90 per cent he'd ask what happened to the other 10 per cent. If I said I came third in my class he'd want to know who came first and second. Personally, I think this is a healthy outlook and it's right that people should strive to be the best they can be.

Suffice to say I did OK in my exam and I then managed to get through the bizarre process that was the practical part of the test. It is a timed assessment where the candidate has to read a pack of information and then interact with a role player. It was false and contrived but it was another hoop to get through.

Having got my exams under my belt, I had a decision to make: whether to go for promotion or leave it for now. I had done just over two years' service and I had no skills or experience in anything other than front-line uniform roles; I had barely scratched the surface of policing. This is where my competitive side got the better of me and I decided that I would put my hat in the ring.

It's strange how, looking back, you remember conversations that now make so much sense. One such discussion took place with a police officer who told me that the higher you go up in the organisation, the less fun you will have. He questioned whether senior officers actually enjoyed their job at all, and certainly whether they had fun. Now, I know that work is not all about having fun but it's not bad to strive for that either, as we spend a huge proportion of our lives at work. He was a PC with almost thirty years on the beat and he clearly still had the drive and motivation to get out there day after day and meet the great British public.

I took the interview board and then got the news that I had been successful and was being promoted. It was an amazing feeling and quite a scary one too. If truth be told, I hadn't expected to get my stripes so I hadn't really thought that hard about what it meant. I was now going to be responsible for managing a team of officers and making those difficult decisions – no longer would I be the one who was able to refer to the sergeant for advice: I *was* the sergeant!

I briefly went to a very rural station just outside Ipswich where I had an experienced team to supervise. Not unusually, it was a beat that had two small stations and I would be based at one of them in Capel St Mary. It was a place that I'd driven past thousands of times as it sits just off the main A12 road to London. The beat itself covered hundreds of square miles of nothing. Welcome to rural Suffolk, again!

I will be honest: I was not happy with the posting, as I had spent a fair amount of my probation in the wonderful Suffolk countryside and I now wanted to be working in Ipswich.

Having said that, I learned an awful lot during my first posting. I was enthusiastic and I came in all guns blazing with ideas about how to be more proactive and more efficient. My first mistake was that I thought I knew best. Who knows, maybe I did, but that was irrelevant. I should have come in, spent some time having a look at the team and how it worked, and then if things needed to be changed I should have done it later in a far more sensitive and measured way.

I remember getting a call from one of the PCs asking for me to meet him and a couple of the other officers on the team. I apprehensively drove over to meet them and it was a very interesting chat and one that I still consider now. They felt that I was treating them like children and micro-managing them. Now, I don't know anyone who genuinely likes getting constructive feedback but that's exactly what it was and I took it on board. On reflection, I had to agree. That was the first lesson of many.

After that posting, I arrived back in Ipswich and took over as sergeant on a response team. I'd only been at Capel St Mary for a month or two so I was delighted to get the chance to get back into the fast lane. This was what I had been working towards and I loved it.

It was fast paced and demanding, really demanding, dealing with critical incidents and supervising a large team of officers. I firmly believe that you should lead by example and from the front. With the greatest respect, anyone can supervise by sitting around completing admin and checking paperwork; I wanted to be standing shoulder to shoulder with the team, doing my part. There is an excellent quote that says 'No individual should take the blame for a loss because no individual should get the credit for a victory.' It was a guy called John Wooden who said it and it's absolutely true; I find it hard to relate to people who constantly refer to 'my team'. Mr Wooden was the head basketball coach for the University of California and he clearly agreed. It's not your team, it's our team.

I'd been on the team for around a year and a half when I got a call out of the blue. The Chief Constable wanted me to go and work for him at Police Headquarters as his staff officer. This was a job that was only ever done by an inspector so I was a little taken aback and even more so because he had asked for me personally. I was very flattered and accepted the offer, starting at Police HQ a few days later. This was going to turn out to be a defining moment for me.

The role of staff officer can be very sought after and generally it is something that is done by people who are looking for promotion and want to get a better insight into the organisation and, to be blunt about it, want to impress the senior management team. I guess that when I arrived that was why I wanted to do it too.

On my first day I met the team of PAs and other support staff within Executive Services and settled down into my new office. The Chief Officer team all met me and I had my first meetings with the Chief Constable. I was now in the slightly strange position of being directly accountable to the Chief.

From the start I was helped hugely by the other staff within Executive Services, who seemed to speak a different language to me and could complete tasks with absolute ease.

Within a day or two, I realised that I had made a big mistake and this was not the job for me. Whenever someone starts a new job there will be some nerves and apprehension, but this seemed different. I'd barely unpacked my belongings and I already knew it was the wrong job in the wrong place at the wrong time.

I remember sitting in my office, which overlooked the main drive at Police HQ, and watching the traffic cars and ARVs going out and thinking: that's what I want to do. It hit me like a train and I felt completely helpless. I was in a really difficult position. I had taken on a job with little or no understanding of what it entailed and now my only option was to stick with it or tell the Chief Constable that I didn't want his job. I decided on the latter option.

The Chief Constable was a man called Alastair McWhirter. He was well liked by officers and was a jovial, personable Scotsman. He had a real knack of putting people at ease and telling funny stories.

He would often be seen around Headquarters or popping into a police station to say hello. I remember one occasion when I was sitting in the sergeants' office at Ipswich getting ready to start a day shift. It was still really early, around 6 a.m., and the night-turn sergeant was struggling; he was sitting back in his office chair, feet on the desk, tie off, stab-proof vest crumpled in a corner and barely able to keep his eyes open.

It was the end of a long night and probably the end of a long week of shifts, and it showed; an unshaven, dishevelled mess! He looked like he'd been on the piss all night. In bounced the Chief, with 'Good morning, chaps!' I have never seen someone go from being half asleep to fully awake and terrified so quickly. In hindsight it was funny but I think the experience probably aged my sergeant colleague.

I wasn't expecting such a humorous encounter as I went into the Chief's office and nervously explained that I really wanted to go back to Ipswich, and that I thought I had made a mistake in accepting the job.

'Sir, I'm really grateful for the opportunity but I want to go back to Ipswich.' I was a twenty-three-year-old lad who was having to make my case to the leader of the entire organisation. I wasn't sure how he would react but I was confident that he'd let me go back. I just hoped he'd be understanding and supportive too.

The Chief sat behind his desk, moved the papers he had been reading to the side and explained how it was going to be: 'You're here until I tell you otherwise so I suggest you get on with the job that you're here to do.' It certainly wasn't an angry exchange but it was to the point and it became a one-way conversation – he spoke and I listened.

I remember leaving the office thinking, *What a complete mess*. I fondly thought back to the team I had left and the fact that I loved my work, and now I was trapped and had nowhere to go.

I spent the next few weeks thinking about my situation. I am one of those people who can be consumed by things and this was one of them. It would be the last thing I'd think about when I closed my eyes and the first thing I'd think about when I woke up. I took counsel from my father and then I made up my mind. I was going to tell the Chief Constable that I wanted to be posted back to Ipswich or I would resign.

My father gave me sound advice: 'Don't ever make a threat that you are not prepared to carry out.' I agreed with that but it wasn't actually that relevant as I was deadly serious. I was ready to resign!

I went and spoke to my line manager in Executive Services; she was really good and understood where I was coming from: in essence the job was just too far out of my comfort zone and it had made me reflect on my career and where I was going with it. She kindly agreed to speak to the Chief on my behalf and she would let me know what he said. I spent a few anxious hours making myself scarce, waiting to hear the news, and then I was told that I would be going back to Ipswich. It felt like a huge weight off my mind, but I was well aware that my reputation might have suffered some irreparable damage.

When I walked back into the office, the Deputy Chief Constable, Colin Langham-Fitt, asked to see me. This was strange as I didn't recall us ever speaking one-to-one during my month in the post, so I guessed that it was probably in relation to my exit. The DCC was an older gentleman who was about to retire from the police and he opened up the conversation by saying that he had been told that I had asked to leave and go back to Ipswich.

He said, 'Some people will say that you have just committed career suicide. Let me tell you, you haven't.' He explained that the majority of people within the senior command team would be gone in the next few years and things move on, people move on, the job moves on. The best advice he gave me was that I had to be true to myself and I had to do what was right for me. He was spot on and I still hold his words of wisdom in high regard.

Some months later, during Chief Constable McWhirter's leaving speech, he gave me a mention. He told the crowd that had gathered to listen to him that I was Suffolk's version of Sergeant Angel from *Hot Fuzz*! I guess that meant we were still friends.

On my arrival back at Ipswich I felt that the DCC was right: I had to be true to myself and, in fact, I had gone too fast, too soon, and now I had some difficult decisions to make. I remember walking into the inspectors' office and speaking to a boss who I trusted and respected greatly. 'How do you go about being demoted?'

The Inspector looked at me rather blankly and then enquired, 'Sorry, who is getting demoted?'

I explained that I wanted to be demoted, I wanted to give up my stripes and go back to being a PC. It became pretty clear, pretty quickly that this was something new and none of the inspectors had heard of a request like this before. It would mean giving up a sizeable chunk of my salary – £9,000 in fact – and being a PC again. The Inspector was excellent and really supportive and within a few hours all the management had heard that I was going back to being a constable. I understood that this was a little unusual but I had made some wrong decisions and been swept along on the crest of a wave, and I'd allowed my competitive edge to get the better of me, but the

DCC was right: you've got to be true to yourself. I wanted to be a front-line all-action police officer, not a staff officer and, in fact, not a sergeant at all, because I wanted to try other things and gain more experience. I have never been one to shy away from making tough decisions and standing by them, and this was one of those occasions.

I returned to the rank of constable and thoroughly enjoyed it. Once again, I was part of the team, not leading the team, and I was able to concentrate on what I was doing, not what everyone else was doing.

One of the key reasons for reverting back was to be part of the Firearms Unit. I had been an Authorised Firearms Officer for a few years but to be a sergeant on the unit would be, in my mind, completely wrong.

As an AFO you had a day job, in my case as an officer working the beat, but I could be called in to help with armed incidents. In truth, these were very few and far between so how could I lead the Firearms Unit as a sergeant having never been a full-time firearms officer? For that reason I wanted to join the team as a PC and that is exactly what I did.

I remember arriving on the team and being introduced to the colleagues I'd be working with. I then had a very strange sensation to get used to, which was being overtly armed in public places. I recall one occasion in a supermarket when I was in there perusing their selection of sandwiches and the guy next to me suddenly noticed the handgun strapped to my leg and literally froze, with his gaze transfixed on it. It seems strange to think it was such a big deal back then but it was, particularly in Suffolk.

There has always been a lot of discussion about police officers in the UK being routinely armed and I for one am completely against it. I think that to have a situation where all of your police officers have to carry a deadly weapon to protect themselves and the public means that you've lost control. Surely legislation is a better way to ensure that guns aren't easily available and, when people are found in possession of them, hammer them for it. No ifs, buts or maybes. Lock them up for a very long time as nobody carries a gun unless they are going to use it. I know that police officers in other areas of the UK may feel differently but I think the current status quo of specialist teams and Armed Response Vehicles seems a good position to be in.

I worked on the Firearms Unit for about three months and during that time it became clear that, after all that I had sacrificed to get my chance, this was not for me either. I was a robust, positive officer who was not bothered at all by confrontation – in fact, I was normally the one leading from the front – but the introduction of a firearm changed all of that. I was suddenly very conscious of it and not comfortable at all. I gave it a few weeks and things just got worse, not better, and it culminated in what was to become my final incident as an Authorised Firearms Officer.

I had been working a week of nights on the ARV with my mentor and just before we were due to knock off at 7 a.m. we got called to an incident where a man was cutting himself with a knife.

My mentor was a lovely man. Dave was one of those people who would capture the attention of a room with his funny, dramatic stories; he had worked in the Met so his tales were always slightly bigger, slightly funnier, slightly better and definitely slightly more far-fetched than anyone else's! He was also someone who never seemed to get too excited about anything

– even when everything was going off, he'd be the same calm and measured guy.

When this particular call came in, we were not far from it, and as we were speeding towards the address, we received an update that a local unit had arrived on scene and was negotiating with the man. As we pulled up, I could see the man stood at the front door, covered in blood and holding a knife. The blood was everywhere, on his hands, arms and face, and he was grasping the knife tightly.

As we got out of the police car, we both drew our Tasers and discreetly held them behind us as we approached. As a police officer, you have lots of different options if talking isn't working – a Taser, incapacitant pepper spray, even your metal baton. This job was perfect for the Taser. We could deliver 50,000 volts from several metres away and it would hopefully allow us time to take control of the knife.

I let my colleague go ahead of me as I was feeling nervous and not confident with this at all. 'Back off or I'm going to do it, I'll kill myself.' He looked deadly serious. After a few minutes the man was becoming more agitated and verbally hostile towards the local officer who was still valiantly trying to calm him down.

'Please put the knife down. We want to try and help you.'

The man began shouting, 'Get SO19 down here now, get them here with their guns, I want them here now.'

This sent thoughts racing through my mind. Was he going to produce a gun and point it at us, hoping that he would be shot? Was this a case of 'suicide by cop', in which the person wants to end their life by being killed by the police? This was the worst possible outcome and I was now on edge, trying to stay calm. The more experienced I had become as a police officer, the fewer were the occasions on which I'd feel as nervous as I did then – my heart was racing, my legs started to shake and it all felt slightly surreal. I was putting all my faith in Dave to sort this one.

After a few moments the man suddenly put the knife towards his neck, shouting that he was going to 'do it'. Without any hesitation Dave raised his weapon, took a step forward and fired it at the man.

'Taser, Taser, Taser!' I heard the pop as the Taser was fired and I could see it hit him directly in the chest. The man went completely rigid like a plank of wood and fell back against the doorframe, totally incapacitated. He began to slide down the wall, unable to break his fall, and he crashed against a mirror, sending glass everywhere. It was like a switch inside me flicked and I ran forward, jumped the low garden fence and grabbed the man.

'Drop the knife, don't move!' I bellowed at him. As the knife fell to the floor, I kicked it away into the bushes. Up until the moment that the Taser was fired, I was motionless and as incapacitated as he was now. After the situation had been resolved, I got back in the ARV and I was in complete admiration of my colleague who had been so decisive.

This incident had made my mind up so I went to see the Firearms Inspector. He was a good, solid boss who took no prisoners but was completely genuine. He had been heavily involved during my initial firearms course, often dropping in to observe the training scenarios or put us through our paces with some circuit training. The whole cohort of wannabe armed officers was somewhat nervous of him. He had the ability to say very little and yet leave you in no doubt what he expected, and woe betide anyone who wanted to argue back or be disrespectful.

Despite this, I felt very comfortable going to see him because he was a good man and a great boss. I explained the issues, and that I felt really uncomfortable in my role and that carrying a firearm had changed my perspective. 'I just don't understand why I felt like that, I just froze.'

He said to me, 'You do realise that I will have no alternative but to take your permit from you today?'

I replied, 'I know, that's what I am here to do,' and placed it on the desk in front of him. A firearms permit is the legal authority to carry a firearm, which, unlike almost anything else in the police, is something that officers can't be made to do. I remember how proud I was the day I got my permit, having passed the course. I left the room wondering how many officers who currently think that cops should be routinely armed have actually thought it through. Could they carry a firearm and still work in the way that we do in the UK? Would they be willing to go through the investigative process that would follow a shooting? I doubt it. I am absolutely full of admiration and respect for our firearms officers; they do an incredibly difficult job and as someone who has seen them up close and personal, I think they are some of the most professional people you could wish to meet.

When I arrived back at Ipswich, I felt like my career was descending into a farce – I had been the staff officer and then left that. I got demoted in order to do firearms and then left that. I was gaining a reputation for being someone who just couldn't settle at anything and perhaps all the good work I had done early on in my career was now being thrown away. I remember speaking to the Superintendent at Ipswich, who was someone I had worked for before and for whom I had the greatest respect. 'What you need, Ali, is a bit of stability.' That was an understatement.

I was put back on a response team and within a year I was sitting my sergeant's interview for promotion – a second time! Lots of people said to me before my interview that it would be a foregone conclusion as I had been a sergeant before. I would always point out that if I took them down to the test centre and got them to retake their driving test it wouldn't be a formality. There was always a chance I'd fail it and I knew that there would be the awkward questions about my previous demotion. I wasn't wrong.

I had the interview and at the end the Chief Superintendent asked me to explain why I had been demoted and why I was now looking to be promoted. I explained to them: I am a man who is willing to make tough decisions, irrespective of what the perception of other people will be, or indeed if the decision has ever been made before. I accepted that I had made some poor choices and perhaps had been too eager to please and had not been true to myself. I also said to them that if you've made a mistake you've got to hold your hands up, take responsibility, take the consequences and then move on. I guess they felt I had convinced them as they promoted me to sergeant. Again.

I never sought promotion beyond sergeant despite applying for the inspector's exams four times and withdrawing four times. I think back to when I joined the police and wanted to go as high and as fast as possible. It felt like to be a success in the police you had to get promoted and become a senior officer. I have completely changed my opinion on this – every public service organisation, and in particular the emergency services, needs highly skilled, highly motivated staff who are at the coal face, delivering that service to the public. The PCs, sergeants and operational police staff are the ones working flat out, trying to make sense of the chaos and doing their very best. They have not risen through the ranks but they are the ones doing the hard yards and holding the line and they all have my respect.

It frustrates me when I think that people only recognise success and status with promotion. I firmly believe that some of our very best people are still working at the lower ranks. Several colleagues spring to mind: a firearms sergeant who transferred from Suffolk to the Met and whom I consider a standout operational firearms officer; a detective sergeant who is as determined as he is tenacious and someone who I'd want to investigate any crime I was the victim of; a recently retired PC who was, for me, the best of the best – conscientious, diligent and the ultimate professional; and a traffic sergeant who is as decent and professional as they come. Top cops doing a top job.

And to anyone reading this, worrying about making a big decision, ask yourself if it is the right decision for you. If it is, then it's the right decision irrespective of what anyone else thinks and, in any case, nothing is for ever.

7

Second chances

It was a mundane Saturday morning in August 2008. I was the duty sergeant covering Ipswich so had walked in to an array of detainees to be dealt with, investigations to be progressed and a whole stack of outstanding items that needed some attention. Saturdays can be like that; you always walk in with a degree of apprehension, hoping that the night shift have not had a tough tour of duty because, if they have, then you can pretty much guarantee that you will. The first few hours would be spent clearing the decks and getting everyone up and running for the day.

After that initial flurry of activity and allocations, the day would often settle down and the mornings would generally be quiet. This day was no different in that respect. Not many emergency calls come in during this time of day so the pressure is off to a degree and there is a predictable lull.

I had decided to go out and about in my police car with nothing specific to do and just see what came in. Just as I was nearing Ipswich town centre, the control room asked for a unit to attend a multi-storey car park following reports of a man being seen standing on the wrong side of the safety barriers on the edge of the top of the building. I knew the location well and wasn't far away so decided that I'd attend and see what was happening. It's not uncommon for the police to receive calls about possible suicide attempts in progress as often there are people working on the roofs of buildings or the witness has mistaken what is actually happening; sometimes, fortunately very rarely, someone is in distress and perhaps thinking of taking their own life.

As I arrived, I parked up and was met by a colleague and dear friend, Ali Maidment. Ali and I had worked together for several years and had become close friends, which is ironic, as I notably told a colleague shortly after Ali arrived on the team that I didn't like him and we'd never get along! There's a lesson there about first impressions, I guess. Ali is someone who I'd trust with my life and I think he feels the same.

Having got there, we both went up to the ninth floor at the top of the building after being let in by security. I soon saw the man in question. It immediately became very clear that this was not a case of a mistaken call or someone carrying out maintenance, this was the real thing.

The car park was privately owned and, unlike most other car parks on a Saturday morning, empty and completely locked up. I said to Ali, 'Wait in the stairwell. I'll have a look and see what I think.'

'Got that,' he replied in typically efficient fashion.

I walked on to the car-park roof, very aware that there were no cars around so, as I approached, the man would see me. I was right: as soon as I set foot on the tarmac, he turned towards me and gestured for me to go away, frantically waving his hand behind him and shouting something. He looked quite elderly, and he was distressed and agitated. I had been a police officer for a number of years and I had encountered lots of people on ledges and bridges. Generally I'd get a feeling for whether they were intent on taking their own life or whether they were relieved the police had arrived. I would never call it attention-seeking because for someone to put themselves in that position they are clearly taking a risk, and it's more often than not an act born out of desperation not attention, and they need support. I have often heard it referred to as a 'cry for help', but I hate the expression; it has connotations of the boy who cried wolf and, with that, complacency could set in. Irrespective of their intentions these are high-stakes, life-at-risk situations and they need to be handled with caution and calm.

This chap looked serious and I noticed that there was a small rucksack near to the safety railings, which he seemed to have left abandoned – it didn't look good at all.

I was now in a conundrum: walk closer and cause yet more anxiety or stand back and give the man some time and space but not be able to talk to him. I stood in the middle of the car park, looking out over the skyline of the town, and everything just seemed to stop. Little did the people below realise what was unfolding above them.

This was the type of situation that was going to test me and our team to the limits. It's also the type of incident where people may want to walk on by and not get involved. Personally, I could never do that: it is someone's father, husband, brother or son, and to do nothing is just not an option. I have always believed it's better to try and fail than never try at all. I called the police control room on my radio. 'Can we get some negotiators on their way? I think we're going to need a bit of help with this.' That was an understatement.

I was still some 50 metres away so I decided to stand my ground but not go any closer. Ali was nearby, stood in a doorway at the top of the stairs as we didn't want to startle the man or force his hand in any way, and we had each other in eye contact.

Ali gestured to me, silently asking if I wanted him to join me; not now, not yet. Other officers were now rushing to the scene but they were to remain on the ground level in case the worst happened.

Then everything just seemed to stop. I couldn't move forward and I wasn't moving back, and it became a waiting game to see how things developed. I was well aware that the crisis negotiators would take some time to arrive but I was desperately hoping that they could get there in time and they could speak to the man to try and save his life. It hadn't gone unnoticed, though, that they would have the same problem I had; we just couldn't get near to him.

After roughly five minutes the man seemed to be getting more animated, he was turning around more often, holding onto the rail and leaning back, and in my opinion he was preparing himself to jump. The odd glance heavenward added to my concern; was he about to do it? I guessed the negotiators might not get to the scene in time after all.

It's at moments like this that you realise that police officers are all just ordinary people but they're doing an extraordinary job. Take a moment to think: what would you do? I was an experienced officer and a sergeant, and yet my stomach was churning and my mind racing. I felt absolutely helpless and the situation was desperate.

All of a sudden the man disappeared beyond the railing and out of my sight, seemingly lowering himself off the side. The time for waiting was over and the time for action was now. I had to try and do something. I shouted to my colleague, 'Ali, he's gone,' and then I began to run towards the edge of the rooftop, fully expecting to see him lying dead on the pavement below.

Much to my amazement, as I got nearer I could see that he was still holding on to the barrier but was now dangling precariously over the edge. I could reach under the barrier towards his left wrist so I grabbed it. Within seconds Ali arrived and I shouted, 'Grab him! Grab him!' Ali grabbed his right arm, which was still holding onto the top rail.

As soon as we had hold of him, he let go and I felt a sudden weight as it jolted through his arm and into my hands, and the man dangled in the air.

Unbeknown to us, the police control room were watching this on CCTV and were also on the phone to one of the crisis negotiators. The control room dispatcher told the negotiator that we'd now reached a critical stage and that the time for talking had gone. It was over to Ali and me to try and save the man's life.

For the next few moments, the man struggled and struggled and then struggled some more, shouting at us to let him go as we were hurting him. He was kicking with his legs in order to throw his body around like a rag doll, and with every jerk and jolt came yet more weight, and my hands and arms were put under even greater strain. I was kneeling on the floor and all I could see was the wrist I was holding.

I remember thinking, *What do you mean, we're hurting you? You're about to die, we're trying to help you.*

He continued to struggle and we continued to fight with all our might to hang on to him.

I shouted over the railings as loud as I could, 'Help, please help us, we can't hold on.' I knew that there were other officers in the street below and now I wished that I'd had a few more on the roof but I never thought we would be in this position.

I'd expected that we would have negotiated with the man, listening to his worries and concerns, and that we would have convinced him to climb back over the railing. Or, he would have jumped. Either way, I never expected to be physically holding him while he was dangling over the side of a nine-storey car park.

After a couple of minutes Ali started to lose his grip, as the man was struggling hard, and in the muggy August air he was sweating profusely; in fact, we were all sweating profusely with the exertion. My colleague desperately tried to maintain his grip, grabbing over and over again as the man's arm slipped through his hands.

All of a sudden, his grip was gone and my dear friend reeled back, half expecting the man to fall. He didn't. We still had a chance and Ali began to heave himself even further over the top of the railings, grabbing whatever he could of the man's clothing to try and re-establish his grip.

I was unaware that Ali had lost his grip at the time and I am glad I didn't know. I just kept holding on – I had a really good grip and I had one job: to keep his wrist in my hands for as long as it took. Easier said than done.

I then noticed that Ali had a hand free so I told him to press the emergency button on the top of my radio. That activates the microphone for ten seconds and no matter who else is talking on the radio channel, it cuts across the top of them. It's seldom used so when it goes off everyone stops and listens, frantically wanting to know where the officer is who needs urgent assistance. If you ask any police officer, they'll say that when they hear those beeps go off, it turns their blood cold – and if it doesn't, it should.

Ali leant down and pressed the small round red button on the top of my radio. 'Please, please help us, we can't hold on much longer, we need help now. If you don't get up here soon, he's going to die.'

My words were desperate and full of anguish. I don't remember what was said by other people on the radio channel. I was now panicking and fighting not for my life but for a man who I did not know and who seemingly wanted us to drop him.

And so it went on and on and on. Ali and I were now not talking to the man, as it was clear that he was in a bad state and intent on struggling free from our grasp whatever we said.

I said to Ali, 'We've got to keep going, no matter how tired we think we are, no matter how desperate we think this is, we must keep going. If we give up and he dies we will always wonder could we have kept going, could we have hung on for another second longer? We can't afford to have any regrets.'

My hands were now getting wet with sweat and my arms were burning hot like I'd never felt before, but I had decided that no matter what, my hands would have to buckle and break before I would let go. I remembered all the times in my squash career when I'd been pushed to the limit and how much further we can go if we just convince ourselves. I could be a stubborn, bloody-minded man at times, and on this occasion that was the perfect way to be.

There is no greater prize than saving a life and I said to Ali that's exactly what we were going to do. 'Come on, man, we're going to do this.' I think we were trying to convince each other but the situation couldn't have been more perilous.

After five long, agonising minutes the backup started arriving and never have I been so relieved to hear cops sprinting towards me. There were suddenly people everywhere, frantically grabbing, grappling and trying to reach the man who was dangling off the edge of the building. I remember lots of shouting.

'I've got him, I've got him.'

'I have his arm.'

'Who's got his belt? Someone get his belt.'

'He's going, he's slipping.'

The relative quiet that had gone before was now complete pandemonium. I was still kneeling on the floor, desperately holding on to his wrist, as I had been since the start – that was my job and I was going to stick to it.

After what seemed like a few minutes, but in reality was a matter of seconds, it became clear that I was now preventing the others lifting him back to safety. 'Sarge, let go, let go, we've got him.'

I needed to be absolutely sure. Imagine what would have happened if we all assumed someone else had him and in fact none of us did and, after all the endeavour, he fell to his death.

I shouted, 'Everyone shut up.' I then went through it all. 'Who has his right arm?'

'I do.'

'Who has his left arm?'

'I do, I've got it.'

'Who has his belt?'

'I've got him, I've got his belt.'

I was far from convinced but it seemed that we had him and we would have no better chance than now to save his life. All the time, he was still struggling and pulling and shouting that we were hurting him.

Once we'd confirmed we had him, I let go and, despite the man making one last effort to pull backwards over the edge, within a flash he was over the railings and safely on the tarmac of the car-park roof.

We immediately handcuffed him behind his back and reassured him, 'You're safe now, you're OK.'

He kept shouting, 'You were hurting me, you were hurting my arms.'

It made no sense. I remember that Ali and I remained completely focused on him. Even when he was on the floor – and he was quite elderly and handcuffed – I was terrified that he would somehow struggle free and run towards the edge again. There was a complete lack of rational thought – but I just couldn't bear the thought that we'd lose him now.

A colleague who had arrived to help suddenly reeled away and sank to their knees, clearly exhausted by the exertion. Another burst into tears and one began retching and trying to be sick.

I was just numb, task-focused but numb. I indicated to the security guy, 'Open your car, get him in there now.' We put the man in the back and he was driven down to the road below us.

Staff from the police control room and also the local authority had watched the whole incident from start to finish. They had lived every minute of it with us, shouting encouragement at the monitor and desperately willing us to succeed – perhaps it was their support that got us over the finishing line.

Once we got to ground level, the man was placed in a police car and taken to hospital. He was clearly still very distressed and very agitated, confused and almost angry about what had happened. He received first-class care from my colleagues, who reassured him with an arm round the shoulder and a hand on his forearm, 'You'll be OK, we'll look after you now.'

I spoke to the security guy again and asked for his mobile number in case we needed to speak to him. It was at this point that I realised the physical toll the last few minutes had taken out of me – I couldn't hold the pen let alone write with it. My arms were completely useless. It's lucky I didn't need to call him back because my attempt at writing was woeful.

The team all headed back to the station and we decided to watch the CCTV in order to debrief the event, in hindsight probably not the best idea. This event changed me. It affected me and my colleagues very deeply.

Initially I had the sheer elation of having helped to save the man's life and the knowledge that his family would be able to spend time with him and hopefully he'd get the support he needed. But there were lots of questions. Why did he not jump? Why did he want us to drop him? Why, despite it being such a positive outcome, did I consider it such a negative experience? How long could we have hung on for? What would have happened if we had dropped him?

I remember many weeks and months later waking up in the middle of the night and the first thing I'd think of would be this incident, running over it time and time again. I lost all interest in my squash – I remember playing a team match and after the first game I walked off court. I didn't want to be there; it seemed so insignificant. Everything seemed so insignificant.

I don't mind admitting it, I was completely traumatised by what we had been through.

Several months later, Ali and I were nominated for the National Bravery Awards and the local press wanted to come and interview us. We went back to the car park but there was no way I could go back on the roof.

As we got to the top of the stairs my blood ran cold, my legs felt like jelly and my breathing quickened. No, not a place I wanted to go. As time has moved on I've become more settled and I think I've recovered from the trauma of this incident, but every time I drive past the car park I can't stop myself glancing up at the ledge and at the CCTV camera that captured the event. It's something I will remember for as long as I live. As for the man, I hope that we gave him that second chance.

8

Tough times need tough people

It's a strange life being a police officer. There are few jobs in the world where everything you do is an attempt to make things better, but invariably you bear witness to some of the worst things imaginable. It's also compounded by what seems to be the unrelenting criticism and scepticism intrinsically linked to being a cop. And perhaps unusually these days this job has got absolutely nothing to do with financial reward, material gain or the bottom line.

It may surprise some people when I say that everything the police do is intended to make things better but I genuinely feel that is the case. Whether it is responding to someone who is under attack, providing emergency first aid to a stranger in the street or arresting someone, it is to protect people from harm, sometimes even from themselves.

I remember taking a child into protective custody after they had been found within a crack house with their drug-addicted parents. Nobody ever goes to work wanting to break up a family and remove a child from their parents, but we did and I'd do the same again tomorrow. The distress written all over that poor child's face, pleading with us to let them stay, will remain with me for a very long time but it was the right thing to do.

I think it's fair to say that some things cops witness are almost beyond comprehension – parents ill-treating their own children, gratuitous violence, blatant acts of dishonesty and a complete lack of morality.

I also never quite comprehended, before I joined the police, the pressure involved in being a police officer. I don't think that it was a conscious effort on my part to ignore it; you are just never exposed to the pressure until you are living it every day, and by then it almost becomes your normality. You learn to put the majority of that to the back of your mind and just keep pushing forward. It's something that you have to accept from the day you join.

I remember being told by my tutor on my very first shift, 'If you're not prepared to make decisions then you're in the wrong job.' He was absolutely right. Other people's lives are in your hands and that's a responsibility that weighs heavy on you legally, morally and emotionally.

Many a day will a cop have gone home still worrying about someone else's welfare and whether they've done the right thing. It frustrates me when I hear people belittle the role of a front-line response officer – no, it's not all about standing outside nightclubs and issuing parking tickets, as more often than not it's about life and death and raw emotion. I think that over a number of years you almost become fatigued from that pressure that you live with; it grinds you down and becomes your normality. It's sometimes only when the pressure is off that you suddenly realise how much you've been under. It's also true that often there are a few cops who have a disproportionate amount of responsibility and pressure resting on their shoulders; I was a response sergeant, tactical advisor, hostage negotiator and a police search advisor. My work was full of life at risk and that is pressure, real pressure, as the stakes are so high.

I wonder what the effects are of witnessing these incidents day after day and the pressure that comes with it. I think that as a service the police have become much better at recognising when colleagues have been subjected to trauma – witnessing death, injury or perhaps a situation when their own life has been in immediate danger. I am not sure, though, that we all fully appreciate the long-term effects of the accumulative exposure to such negativity and pressure.

I am sure I'm not alone when I feel that I lived two parallel lives – one that was full of kindness and happiness and one that absolutely was not. It can distort your view of the world and it makes you sometimes question humanity as a race.

But then things will happen that make you realise that the good far outweighs the bad, the light is far brighter than the dark, and optimism and hope are more powerful than anything else: the actions of the minority can never overshadow the endeavour and kindness of the majority. A simple acknowledgement of the work police officers do and the gratitude of the public can be the spark that keeps cops going during tough times.

I had been a front-line police officer for almost two decades and I had seen things that people should never see, some of which will never leave me. Patrolling around I would pass significant locations every day that reminded me of some of the most tragic events I've had to deal with. Has it changed me? Yes, irreversibly and profoundly. Does it make me appreciate the good things that little bit more? Of course.

The challenge we face is to motivate police officers to tackle these acts head on and not shy away from them. I am not ashamed to admit that over the whole of my service I had moments when I felt battle weary and just wanted to walk away and enjoy the other part of my life, but that's what makes police officers who they are. Society relies on the police to ensure that they don't have to be exposed to the things that they are exposed to, and, when they are, the cops are there to protect them, comfort them and help them through it. Police officers are the buffer and, trust me, some days it felt like it. Did I do it for the money? Definitely not. Did I do it for the greater good? Absolutely. I would often tell the team, 'Tough times need tough people,' and cops are some of the very toughest I know.

No matter how tough cops are, though, during these times it is a lonely place and it can feel that nobody actually cares about the police at all. I know that isn't the case but when it feels that the overwhelming majority of coverage is negative and critical, it certainly takes its toll. Unfortunately for the police the greatest support comes from the silent majority. Deep down, we know it's there but we just don't hear it.

9

Succeed as a team or fail as individuals

I CAN SAY WITHOUT any hesitation that the best part of my service has been working on a response team. For the majority of the public who don't think we just hand out parking tickets, this is what they envisage police officers doing: responding to incidents and investigating crime.

There will be those, both inside and outside of the police, who consider this to be the starting point for people who join the police, and then you look to progress and get promoted or specialise. I never saw it like that; for me this was the best and most challenging role within the job. Response officers are the ones who have to deal with whatever life throws at them and literally use what they've got, start where they are and do what they can. There is no such luxury of saying, 'Sorry that isn't in our remit,' and when others are running away, generally it's the response teams who are running forward.

Most officers will say it's not a specialist role; I disagree, as it's probably the most specialist role there is. Officers encounter anything and everything from critical incidents, serious violence, murders, suicides, fatal road traffic collisions, domestic violence, hate crime, safeguarding vulnerable people, missing persons, public order, arresting offenders – the list goes on and on and on. For me that was always the appeal as it meant that you were in the middle of everything big that happened. I don't necessarily agree, though, when I hear cops say that no two days are the same; they may not be identical but they are pretty similar and as time went on there were fewer and fewer times when something happened that made me sit up and contemplate the exceptional nature of it.

When you work on a response team you have to really work together and as a sergeant you feel very responsible for the team dynamic. I truly believe that you succeed as a team or you fail as individuals. I'd love to know what people I worked with really thought of me: I have an idea what they might say but I'll never know for sure. I think they will have thought I had high standards, I wouldn't suffer fools gladly and I wanted to get results. I hope that they also felt I was a kind and caring boss who would move heaven and earth for them.

I believe that when you get promoted and work on a team you begin to forge your own style. It's undoubtedly influenced by other sergeants you've seen and also your own personality and beliefs.

From day one I wanted the team to work together and be positive; I hate negativity, not because I live in my own world where we can achieve whatever we set out to do, but because I'd rather try and fail than never try at all. It's a bit like that game against the Argentinean at the World Championships from my teens: I was out on my feet and felt that I had nothing left in the tank but I actually had more than I thought.

I also think that some of the team would see me as a little fierce at times. I can accept that and I definitely felt that respect was important – not in a pedantic or arrogant way, but we worked in a disciplined organisation dealing with incidents full of threat and risk; we needed a clear chain of command and at times that meant being less than diplomatic and being a bit more direct.

Working on a response team also meant that I had to get used to shift work. Shifts in the police can vary but the commitment is 24/7, 365 days a year. I worked a variety of shift patterns but for the majority of my service I worked six shifts on, four shifts off. I'd start with two early shifts, basically ten-hour days, followed by two evenings finishing between midnight and 4 a.m., and then two full nights starting at 11 p.m. and finishing the following morning. They said that was better for us as it meant that the body clock was moving in the same direction and there were no quick turnarounds from an evening to a day or anything daft like that.

The most challenging shifts were always nights and they definitely got harder the older I got. That 4 a.m. feeling when your body just says no! I can see why the research suggests that shift work kills you because it certainly felt like that. It also meant that I lived my life in ten-day cycles, so the days of the week didn't have much relevance and weekends became pretty meaningless.

When I first started as a sergeant I had a team that was not that well thought of and perhaps lacked the spark or buzz that I wanted. Teams in Ipswich generally had a mix of officers – at one end of the spectrum you had cops who were brand new and had been posted to the town to get their first taste of policing and, at the other end, there were officers who had been policing for years.

The mix of experience made for some interesting dynamics. The younger officers in service would look forward to a new arrival as that would mean that they'd move up the pecking order. I think, in truth, some of the old sweats grew a little tired of the constant stream of young and excitable probationers arriving.

As with most response teams in the police, though, the line-up went through changes and I was lucky to get some new, young officers on my first team who were not only dead keen but were also highly talented.

It was a chance to change the ethos of the team and I then needed to think how to go about that. I was always someone who was happy to lead from the front and try to set the example, and that most certainly set the tone. We were going to be a can-do team who would not back down in the face of aggression or hostility but would be professional and efficient in our work.

On any team you'd get officers who were better suited to some incidents than others. It was the source of many conversations; should officers all do a bit of everything or should you keep round pegs in round holes? First and foremost, I wanted to make sure that as a team we could look after each other and that meant having enough cops who could handle themselves. It was my insurance policy and it made me feel more at ease. When a colleague called for backup, I expected the cars to arrive and for anyone thinking of kicking off to take one look at them and think again.

As the months went by the need to use force went down and down because I think that the criminals we dealt with realised when the game was up. The size of the teams varied over the years too but Ipswich was the biggest town in Suffolk so we always had the lion's share of the county's resources. If we needed to show a bit of force then we would have plenty to put on display.

Over time the team developed and it became a great place to work, with like-minded individuals doing exactly what the public would expect: tackling crime and protecting them from harm.

I remember reading a speech* that Colonel Tim Collins MBE gave to his troops during the Iraq War:

> We go to Iraq to liberate not to conquer. We will not fly our flags in their country. We are entering Iraq to free a people and the only flag which will be flown in that ancient land is their own. Show respect for them. There are some who are alive at this moment who will not be alive shortly. Those who do not wish to go on that journey, we will not send. As for the others I expect you to rock their world . . .

Some of the sentiments from the speech were what I wanted our team to strive for. We should be respectful, and to those who we have no business with we should leave them well alone. However, those who are violent, dangerous, prolific criminals, we should 'rock their world'. I believe that's what the public expect from their police officers; we were the people they entrusted to keep them safe and that starts with front-line response teams.

Also, I was still deeply affected by the loss of my friend and colleague, Cheryl, and that undoubtedly had a huge impact on my psyche. I wanted to ensure that we all started the shift together and we all went home together. Nobody would be left behind.

I also remember reading a lot about how many crimes we solved and how this was a vital performance indicator. To an

* Collins, T, *Rules of Engagement: A life in conflict* (Headline, 2005)

extent, I could understand why because our job is to lock up offenders when they commit crimes, but I wasn't so sure that this necessarily instilled confidence in the public or even if it was something that we should be concentrating on. As a member of the public, I wouldn't necessarily feel more or less reassured if the solved rate was higher or not, but if I called the police because someone was trying to break into my house I wanted to see blue lights and hear screeching tyres coming round the corner at a moment's notice. What's more, I'd expect the cops to be ready for anything; that would give me confidence.

I also thought back to my sporting days and how it was so important not to focus on the result but to focus on performing well. You have no control over the result so all you can do is play to the best of your ability and make sure that you do things right. This was so true of policing and was far more relevant to officers on the front line, rather than telling them to improve their solved rate.

Responding to incidents and crimes in progress was our area of business and by being really positive in the way we responded we'd get the results anyway. I lost count of the times that members of the public, who had called us absolutely terrified, were so grateful when we arrived en masse and ready to keep them safe.

That, for me, was a major part of our team's ethos and something that I'm very proud to have been a part of. We'd work as a team and although everyone would bring their own unique set of skills and experience, there was an expectation that everyone would be positive and dynamic.

It's interesting how a team will change over the years and I was very conscious that would happen. There was no way that we'd keep the same officers year after year.

I think that response policing is brutal both physically and mentally, and eventually it wears people down. I had seen too many cops on response teams who were older in service and the fire had gone out and they were coasting along. I didn't want a team that coasted along; I wanted our team to fly along at 100 mph and tackle things head on.

I have had many a conversation with colleagues bemoaning the lack of experience on response teams and the fact that as soon as officers get the experience and are really competent they move on. I would rather have had a team of officers with fewer than five years' service who were keen, motivated and willing to learn than a team of officers with fewer than five years before retirement. I don't say that in a critical way, because they've done their shift already, but energy is so important to make it all tick.

I thought long and hard about how to get that consistent performance in a constantly changing team, and I decided that the things I could control were my supervision and the team ethos and ethic. It's a bit like the great football teams; the managers often stay the same so the style and feel of the team are constant despite players coming in and out. I wanted to strive for that.

Another aspect of my supervision was that I wanted to be part of the team. Yes, there needed to be respect for rank and a professional working relationship but the team spent more time together than they did with their families and loved ones. I wanted them to arrive at work with a smile on their face and I wanted them to leave with a smile on their face. Work should be a sociable place to come and spend time with friends, and, yes, we'd work bloody hard as well.

Like almost every police team, we'd start the day with a briefing. This was a chance to update the team with key or significant events, share intelligence and recap on anything from the previous shift that was noteworthy.

Every sergeant briefs differently and there will be merit in all the different ways, but for me this was the team talk before we took to the field so it was going to be punchy and businesslike. I expected people to arrive in good time and be ready to deploy at a moment's notice. It always felt like it was us taking the baton from the preceding shift and we were the reinforcements coming over the hill so we had better be ready.

Our team got into a routine of briefing ten minutes before the hour. Some who are reading this will not agree and feel that you're paid from the hour so why start early? It was something we did to get on the front foot so we were ready and waiting. It's also because I think that whenever public service becomes about giving the bare minimum then we're in real trouble. The British Army is respected the world over because its members are the best of the best, they don't give the bare minimum, they excel, and why should that be different for the police? I have no doubt that there are challenges within the military and things aren't perfect but I guess it's about having that can-do, positive mentality.

I recall that after many years of this there was some apparent unrest and I was made aware that 'people were not happy'. I spoke to the Inspector about it and we agreed that we'd advise the team that, as people were not happy, we'd revert back to the hour. For me this was really disappointing but we were a team and the good grace of starting early was not something we could enforce.

The Inspector informed the team and made it clear that the next day we would be starting on the hour. The following day I went into the briefing room to set up and the team were in there, ready and waiting. I called the Inspector and we started ten minutes early. The Inspector finished the briefing by telling everyone that we would be starting on the hour the next day and he really meant it this time.

The following shift I arrived to set up and everyone was in there, ready and waiting. That was the last time we ever discussed the briefing time with that team! For me, that is testament to them wanting to be better and strive for excellence; response teams should do exactly that. And suffice to say, those officers who had raised the concerns in the first place, were happy to say nothing and acquiesce with their teammates.

It's interesting when you think about what others think of the team and how others view you as a sergeant. I was well aware that people felt it was *my* team but I was always of the view that it was *our* team. It's true that as a sergeant you will be a decision maker and sometimes you will have to put your foot down, but it's also important that you spend more time listening than you do talking. I was very lucky that the majority of the team would let me know how things were and if there were any bumps appearing on the horizon.

One such bump was in relation to the deployment of officers in Ipswich. Generally, the cops had a beat and they would work that same beat every day – it meant that they could build up some local knowledge and get to know who lived and worked on their patch. It also meant that you could match the right personalities and experience to the right beat. There were some pretty rough, tough parts of Ipswich and I wanted to have people in those locations who could handle it and not be overwhelmed.

After many years of this model some people on the team raised that they were not enjoying this arrangement and they wanted to change beats and not work the same place all the time; variety is the spice of life after all. I was not convinced and neither was the other sergeant but we agreed that we would trial it for three months to see how it went. We laid down the gauntlet; they needed to show that same desire and improve their knowledge of all the areas in the town. Challenge accepted!

After a few weeks it was clear to see that the team were right; they were more motivated and they were more engaged. After a month we had a chat and we agreed that the trial wasn't necessary and we'd implement the changes. I'm not too proud to accept when I am wrong, and on this issue I had been wrong.

That's part of being a team as well: we have all got to be able to admit when we're wrong and see that as a positive, not a negative.

Over the years I wanted the team to have confidence in each other and the last thing I wanted was to have to be constantly pestering them to do things. On the whole, I didn't need to and I credit that to the senior officers on the team who did a hell of a lot of that for me. I'd regularly hear a PC telling another PC what was expected or helping them improve what they had done. That was music to my ears; if I was the manager of the team, they were the captains on the pitch and they were the ones pushing things along.

I'd sometimes enlist their help to sort out a minor issue; particularly punctuality. As anyone who knows me will tell you, don't be late! It's not about being picky but we were a response team so turning up late didn't really work. If we did have the odd issue with punctuality, I'd ask one of the more senior PCs to have a word. The reason I'd do that is because it would kill two birds with one stone; the officer who had been late would get some friendly advice about timekeeping from a team mate and the senior PC would get the kudos for helping out their less-experienced colleague.

After a time I'd have senior PCs updating me about what they had sorted and, for me, that meant we were a team who were looking out for each other. The problem is that those senior leaders on the team are also the hardest officers to hang on to so you constantly have the worry that you could lose them at any time. I'd never stand in the way of an officer who wanted to move on and try something new but I also could not stand by and just let them walk out the door. I sometimes saw the gusto with which other supervisors and managers supported their colleagues' applications and secretly thought, *Do you actually want shot of them?* To me that would be disrespectful as it would almost suggest that they had little or no value to the team. Many a time I'd have conversations with officers who were wrestling with their own thoughts of whether to move on or stay put; they loved the team and desperately wanted to stay but they wanted to try something new. Over the years they all move on eventually and with my full support, but they would always be an honorary member of the team and know the part they had played.

I think the biggest factor in making sure a team worked as a team was to make things fair. Nothing causes divisions in this world more than when things are unjust or unfair. I was determined to remove that from our team. We made the decision that everyone would carry a workload, everyone would help with constant supervisions and, yes, everyone would even take their turn to work on the front counter at the police station.

It was interesting to see the affect this had; some people weren't best pleased but the majority who were genuine team players realised that to be a team, you can't have a situation where some people are given a higher value than others.

It also showed that if everyone shared the workload and worked together there wasn't an insurmountable amount of work.

And it's the little things that make a difference. We would all start together and, if at all possible, we would all finish together; if that meant everyone was ten minutes late instead of a couple of people being several hours late, then that's what we'd do.

The end of a shift is often quite hectic as officers return to the station with a stack of stuff to sort out – inputting investigations on the computer, booking-in property, submitting intelligence and, importantly, having a catch up with their colleagues. As a sergeant my inbox would fill up almost as quickly as I could empty it with work needing to be reviewed and rubber stamped.

Nothing kills an officer's love of the job more than being the one who is left behind at the end of a shift time after time. Our team was never like that: if people came back and had a stack of stuff to do then everyone would take some of it and get cracking. And nobody would go home until we'd done everything possible to get it done. It made me feel very proud to be part of the team.

Credibility. It's a word that I'd hear bandied about time and time again. For me, credibility has nothing to do with words and has everything to do with actions. Every organisation and company has people who can talk the talk but can't walk the walk. In policing, that is even more important due to the risky and sometimes unpleasant nature of what we do. I'd never have asked a PC on the team to do something that I was not prepared to do myself.

As a sergeant it was also vital to make sure I was there during any really tense and challenging incidents; it gives the team confidence that it will all go to plan.

I remember going to a fatal road traffic collision on the A14.

It came in early one morning when we were on nights and it sounded horrific. A baby had been thrown from the vehicle and the driver, sadly, had been pronounced dead at the scene.

I had every confidence in the team that they would do an amazing job but it was important that, as the leader, I also went. When I arrived it was exactly as I imagined; officers were sorting the road closures, giving first aid, reassuring the public, securing the scene; it was like a finely oiled machine in full swing and I had nothing to do.

My role was to be there for them, to see them in action and support them in delivering a top-quality service in the most difficult of circumstances. When it had all been dealt with and I sat down with the team, we were able to have a debrief and make sure that everyone was OK. Incredibly, the lorry that had come across the wreckage in the road somehow managed to screech to a halt just a few feet before hitting the baby as it lay motionless in the carriageway. Miraculously the infant suffered no serious injuries.

I just don't believe you can lead a team from behind a desk; you have to see what they see, hear what they hear and feel how they feel, and I defy anyone to argue otherwise. For me, leading from the front line gives you credibility.

I've worked with some amazing bosses over the years and, on reflection, I can imagine that I was a right pain in the arse to supervise. I refused to take my leave, I would run out of my appraisal meetings at the slightest hint of an urgent call or even a non-urgent diary appointment, and apparently, according to almost all of those bosses, I am fairly strong willed.

I remember one particular boss who managed to trick me into a meeting to talk about my personal development and then promptly sat between me and the door so I couldn't escape before we'd completed the paperwork!

My very best bosses were not managers, they were leaders. They encouraged the team to be the very best they could be and they had the skills and mindset to eke out every last bit of energy from the cops under their command.

I was also very lucky to have been influenced by some magnificent commanders when I was young in service; they commanded respect and got it from everyone. I owe them a great deal for their support, guidance and counsel over the years.

I think the other part of being in such a demanding role is you've got to have fun. We would deal with some of the harshest, most tragic things, plus we were all taking risks on a day-to-day basis. There must be a chance to unwind and relax, and when handing over to the oncoming team, that was often the time to let off some steam.

The police are known for playing pranks on each other and having some fun. Much of it is childish, mindless silliness but it is a key part in keeping a young, motivated team firing on all cylinders.

And I can assure you that if cops aren't working hard or having fun then there's only one other thing they will do and they do it really well – moan!

There are people who I have worked with over the years who I would literally trust with my life. There are others that I wouldn't, but they are few and far between. You gain this almost unique relationship where you feel incredibly responsible for them and protective of them, but you also have to hold them to account and make sure that they maintain high standards.

Once we set the standard it became far easier to maintain as we had something to lose, we had our reputation to uphold and nobody wanted to let the team down.

10

A monster

When I first joined the police as a special constable, I was introduced to 'Night-Time Economy' or public order policing. For anyone who is not within the industry this basically means policing the pubs and clubs.

Now as someone who has always been teetotal and has never drunk even a sip of alcohol, it was a fairly rude awakening. I remember standing outside a nightclub in Ipswich and it was mind boggling; people who could barely stand up, people who couldn't stop throwing up and people who couldn't stop acting up! It's funny, because this is what is positively referred to as a 'vibrant' night-time economy. Vibrant, no; vile, at times most definitely. But it's wrong to say that it's all like that because we all know that a busy, bustling town centre is a great place to go out and socialise with friends.

Even after almost two decades in the police I'd still get nervous before public order shifts. I think it's because the risk to officers is high, as often situations develop very quickly and you have to think fast and really work as a team.

I've seen officers knocked out, kicked, punched, and even spat at and bitten, so it can be unpredictable. I also think that public order policing is about setting the tone, in the same way that so many other things in life are; it's about those first impressions.

I wanted our team to be friendly and approachable and to enjoy night-time economy policing, but if you had come looking for trouble then you'd find it with us. We were not for backing down and, if people wanted to be aggressive and violent, then we'd tackle that head on.

It's a real art to police public order well and over the years I worked with some amazing cops who just got it. They were able to hold a conversation with a friendly drunk who wanted their picture taken, while also keeping an eye on someone in the queue who was starting to push people's buttons.

They were long nights but if you got back at the end of it and there had been no serious violence or disorder, and there were just a handful of drunks in the cells sobering up for minor offences, then you'd had a great shift.

I got my first taste of public order policing in Leiston. It's a quirky little place built around the expansion of the nearby nuclear power station and, just like any other town of its size, it had some colourful characters.

On one of the first public order nights I worked we were called to a fight in the high street outside one of the handful of pubs in the town. When we arrived a few moments later there was indeed a scrap going on involving a group of about four or five people. (Any cop reading this will be aware, generally when a report comes in of twenty people fighting there's actually only a handful involved and the others consist of passers-by, avid spectators and hangers on.)

As we tipped up to this fight there was a moment that was almost surreal when the blokes throwing punches and kicks at each other paused, realised the police had arrived, and then decided to join forces and direct all their aggression and fury at us!

Not surprisingly, we decided to let the heat come out of it all and as everyone now seemed happy to kiss and make up, we'd wait for a few more officers to arrive.

The predictable Mexican stand-off ensued with the group on the other side of the road, gesturing and jeering. They were clearly not going to back down or disperse and they wanted to let us know that we were not welcome. This went on for a while before eventually fizzling out as they finally wandered off into the night.

Having since worked in a large town with a far bigger night-life, this small-town mentality is certainly not replicated in bigger places and, far from bringing warring factions together, I've spent the last fifteen years having to drag people apart and stop them kicking the living daylights out of each other.

You may think that the night-time economy seems a pretty dark, violent place, but that is not always the case; it can also be a very funny and interesting environment in which to work. I remember one particular incident involving a call from the CCTV operators reporting a large fight in a car park in town. The usual questions came raining down on them. Descriptions? Weapons? Direction of travel?

Often the information you get back is vague even though the operators in the control room skilfully manipulate the cameras to get the best angle and keep track of the main troublemakers as they sprawl in all directions. No such problem this time as, much to my amusement, the descriptions were, for once, particularly distinctive. Friar Tuck and Robin Hood were giving the Three Musketeers a right good kicking!

Armed with these indisputable descriptions the team leapt into action and a short time later the custody corridor was filled with men in tights all looking a little dishevelled and very embarrassed. What was even more amusing was the thought that the following day they'd all be released from custody; fancy dress isn't quite as funny when it's mid-afternoon on a cold winter's day.

Around six weeks later I was walking through custody and I noticed a guy who looked really familiar but I just couldn't quite place him. This isn't unusual in our job as we meet hundreds of people on a weekly basis.

I walked through a second time but I still couldn't pin down where I'd seen him, although he seemed to know me as he acknowledged me both times. On the third walk down the corridor, it all came back to me. I stopped and tentatively said, 'Were you Robin Hood?'

'No,' he replied sheepishly, 'I was Friar Tuck.' He accepted his police caution and I am sure he learnt his lesson through the sheer embarrassment alone.

There will be people who feel that the police are over the top with public order policing and end up nicking people who are fundamentally decent but who have just had too much to drink. This is a dilemma that I have considered many, many times and I can only speak from my own experience: sometimes you've got to be cruel to be kind.

I recall one example many years ago where a young lad was in town and had got to the stage where he was drunk and he was starting to get involved with people he didn't know. He would bump into people as he staggered up the street, he fell against some shop windows and almost broke them, and he then got into an argument with someone in the kebab shop.

Now none of this is particularly heinous – far from it – but as a police officer I could see where this might end up. This lad could accidentally bump into a woman walking the other way and knock her over, quickly followed by her boyfriend knocking him out. He could fall straight through a window and severely injure himself; he could fall in front of a car or even into the docks. He could get so enraged with the person in the kebab shop that he lost his senses and started a fight.

All of these are bad outcomes and will result in him either being a victim of crime, severely injuring himself or becoming an offender. Our only option was to arrest him.

I can also recall another incident involving a teacher who was in a similar position and he was just not for calming down. I always found that if someone wouldn't listen to their friends who were telling them to chill out and go home then the chances are it had gone too far.

A colleague and I intervened and spoke to the teacher, and he was as obnoxious and unpleasant as anyone else I'd dealt with that night. 'Haven't you got anything better to do? Why don't you go and arrest some murderers and rapists? Fucking jobsworth!'

Not surprisingly he got locked up for the night. On a more positive note, he walked out of custody the following day all in one piece. Oh, and he had to pay a fixed penalty notice for being drunk and disorderly. That's not ideal for a teacher, but compared to becoming the victim of a serious violent crime, dying as a result of being hit by a car or being sent to prison for causing grievous bodily harm, this was by far the lesser of those evils.

I always used to consider what I would want the cops to do if it was my friend or family member: if it meant that they came home in one piece and had been stopped from making a life-changing decision, I'd want them to get nicked as well.

Having said that, our team did have one secret weapon. As far as I'm aware, no other team at Ipswich had something similar; in fact, I'm not sure if I've ever seen one like it anywhere else.

We had an officer we could deploy at a moment's notice and invariably he could sort out almost any hint of over exuberance single handed. He didn't need a gaggle of officers to help him, he was a one-man band. I can't give his real name because he still works for the police but his operational callsign was the 'Fun sponge'.

At the slightest inkling of people having fun, he would be sent over to soak it all up and that would be the end of that. People were not going to have fun with him around. He'd literally suck the life out of it! I am not even really sure how he did it, perhaps it was the way he carried himself, or the conversations he didn't want to get involved in. Whatever it was, it was highly effective.

I remember one particular evening when he got into an argument with some squaddies outside a bar and, in the end, we all got in the police cars and left him to it. Even the squaddies were asking if they could come with us.

All joking aside, he was one of the best officers we had; I guess he just didn't like dealing with drunks and he had a knack for calming things down or winding things up, but invariably it wasn't much fun any more. We often smile about it now and occasionally we'll reminisce about the 'fun sponge' being deployed!

The other thing that public order policing seems to do is bring out the argumentative side of people. I do understand that it can be incredibly frustrating that you've been refused entry because you've been sick all down your front, you have no ID and you've then threatened to knock out the door staff, but no matter how much you debate the point, you're still not getting in. And no, I don't give a shit if your father knows the Chief Constable!

I didn't mind allowing people to vent their frustrations but don't take the piss and whatever you do don't start threatening people. I remember one incident where a young lad had been ejected from one of our biggest nightclubs. Policing can be very animalistic at times; do I think this person poses a threat to me and, if so, how big is that risk?

Well, when we arrived he was a young lad but he was a big lad. He towered over me (and I'm six foot three) and he was probably well over twenty stone, so suffice to say he did pose a big risk and he looked well up for a row.

I strolled over and, after being given the circumstances by the door staff, I explained to the lad that he was not going to be able to get back in and perhaps it was time to head home. Unfortunately, he wasn't ready to go home yet and he left me in no doubt that this was going to get messy. Contrary to what people may think, I, along with most cops, don't go to work to be threatened or assaulted.

This guy was a monster! Here was a young, strong, aggressive drunk giant of a man who was so angry and fuelled up on beer that he wanted to tear it up with someone.

Fortunately for the other people in that club, it ended up being us, not them. I told him, 'Listen, you're either going home or you're getting nicked.'

A few moments later, after the inevitable punch up, he was locked up. I remember walking away from that night thinking that to bump into that guy in a nightclub or pub would be my worst nightmare – no equipment, no team of officers to help and no training. That's why, for me, public order policing is so important and, together with licensees and security staff, we need to create a safe environment for people to socialise in. If that means locking up the violent, aggressive ones, then let's get on with it.

People will have seen police officers trying to arrest people in these situations and it always looks messy. And that's because it is: it's really messy. Our objective was to try and 'get control', which normally meant restraining the arms and applying handcuffs. That sounds simple but when it turns into a violent game of Twister with arms and legs everywhere, it's really not simple at all.

Invariably it ends up on the floor and, believe it or not, that is often the safest place for it to be, accepting that it puts cops in a pretty vulnerable position for a few moments. I remember one incident where officers decided that a guy was so violent that they were going to apply Velcro leg restraints to stop the detainee kicking out or injuring officers. Much to my colleague's surprise, he realised it was his legs that were now strapped together and he was the one unable to get up! To be fair, they both had black trousers on.

The other aspect of public order policing is just how vulnerable people become when they are out on the town and things don't go to plan. It never ceases to amaze me how many young men and women will walk home in the wee small hours when heavily intoxicated and often not dressed for the weather. The risks are there and they are undeniable, yet people will consistently take them.

It caused me a lot of frustration because the last thing I ever wanted to deal with was someone who had been seriously assaulted, robbed or even raped. To know that people were at risk would cause me genuine concern.

I worked on a number of really effective operations and initiatives to try and help make things safer, and I think that everyone would agree that the situation now is far better than a few years ago. People do tend to stick with friends and plan their way home and, on the whole, venues are far more responsible and identify when people are vulnerable. Unfortunately, though, this work will never be done as there will always be risk takers and offenders who try and take advantage.

11

One life

THERE CAN BE nothing more valuable than life itself. Irrespective of whether you are of faith or no faith, life is the currency of our existence but it should never go up or down in value as there is nothing more precious.

Having said that, I wonder if society has become almost desensitised to the loss of life – hundreds of people dying in a tragedy many thousands of miles away is almost daily news and yet lost behind the headlines. Every one of them is another human being. It's interesting when you sit back and think about what the crises are that we encounter in our daily lives; a water leak at home, a car that won't start, a road network paralysed by a bit of snow or perhaps being late for an important meeting. Inconvenient? Yes. Crisis? No, not really. And I guess, as with most things, it's all about perspective: it's probably not the end of the world.

Being a police officer, you see life in high definition with surround sound, and sometimes I wished that we could turn down the resolution slightly. But it's also an occupation that puts you in a position where you can save lives and that is the greatest privilege and honour of them all.

As police officers, we'd spend a huge amount of time trying to prevent harm and sometimes, more often than you'd perhaps think, save a life. The ultimate goal is to look after people and keep them safe. Perhaps it's safeguarding a victim of domestic violence, talking a suicidal person off a ledge or apprehending a violent attacker before they commit a heinous crime.

Unfortunately, though, sometimes the harm has already been done.

I remember one particular incident where a colleague and I were called to attend a stabbing near to the town centre. It was in an area of the town that I knew well, a narrow street of terraced houses.

When the call came in, we were seconds away from the location and on our arrival we were met by a scene of sheer panic. We turned into the street and could see the road was filled with people. They had clearly heard the sirens approaching so some of them immediately began waving at us and beckoning us towards the victim. The man lay on the pavement right outside the open front door of a house. There were people standing around him, horrified and in shock.

It's the strangest feeling because as a cop you sense when things are serious or, as in this case, really serious. Maybe it's the non-verbal signals that we all give off as humans, or that sixth sense that tells us when life is at imminent risk.

As we ran towards the crowd I had that feeling in the pit of my stomach that this was grievously bad. We rushed to the aid of the victim, who was conscious and alert, almost matter of fact about what had happened. 'I've been stabbed. They've stabbed me in the legs.'

He was right, he had been stabbed multiple times in the back of his legs. Having exposed the wounds it became clear, although he may not have realised it, that his life was quite literally ebbing away over the pavement. Ironically, with every beat of his heart his life was in more and more peril. Where were the offenders, some may ask? I didn't care, it was irrelevant. There was only one priority – save this man's life.

It's strange to think that his life, and in some manner the life of all those who cared for him, was now hanging in the balance; the next few minutes would change the course of their very existence, for ever. And even more strikingly, they were now relying on us.

At times like these I would remember a particular saying, 'Start where you are, use what you've got, do what you can.' It's absolutely true. It's no good pondering what kit we wish we had or what else we would want to know or who else we wanted to be with us. The time is now, so get on with it.

I shouted to a lady, 'We need more towels, bring as many as you can find.' She turned and ran back inside the house.

We desperately tried to stem the bleeding but it wasn't working, it was having almost no effect at all and everything was drenched in blood. I remember thinking how much blood there was and it just kept coming like a never-ending stream. He was bleeding out in front of our very eyes.

I realised that the direct pressure wasn't working and that we now had very little time to save this man's life. I said to my colleague, 'I don't understand. Where is all the blood coming from?'

We cut the rest of his jeans off and then we realised he had another stab wound, far more serious than all the others, and the blood was pumping out of him fast. *Fucking hell, he's going to die.* Fortunately, I stopped myself from saying that out loud.

I turned to my colleague who was kneeling next to me. 'I think we need to tourniquet it. We just can't stop the bleeding.'

I removed the man's belt and I pulled it around his leg as tightly as I possibly could, straining on it until it felt like it was going to snap. This technique can be fraught with risk but we had no alternative, with every second that passed he was becoming weaker and weaker and weaker. He was now almost completely unresponsive.

'Come on, fella, stay with us, keep talking to us. You're going to be OK.'

My colleague tried to reassure him too, 'The ambulance will be here any second, mate, just stay awake.'

We both realised how perilously close he was to dying.

At an incident such as this everyone has a job, nobody should be stood by watching – meet the paramedics, close the road, get medical supplies, identify a landing site for the air ambulance.

As such there is a buzz of activity as people rush around, doing whatever they can to help. A PC came running over and put his hand on my shoulder, 'Sarge, what do you need?'

'We need the fucking ambulance!' I shouted.

The ambulance crew arrived eight minutes after we had got there and within seconds he was on his way to hospital with his life still hanging by a thread. At moments such as these, it's as though the person is walking a tightrope between life and death. A police officer's job is to reach out a hand and help them keep their balance, to stop them falling.

It takes far brighter and better qualified people than the likes of me to stop a person dying but we need to buy them time and, with it, hope.

After the ambulance had left, my colleague and I sat in our police car, covered in the blood of someone we'd never met but who we had done everything in our power to save. I said, 'I'm just not sure. He didn't look great at all. I think it's going to be close.'

We both desperately hoped and prayed that he would survive. And he did. We were in the right place at the right time with the right training and the right determination to help save a life. But afterwards there was no great outpouring of emotion or celebration, more a quiet moment of reflection at what might have been and a real sense of accomplishment of a job well done. And then we moved on. In no way does that diminish what had just happened – everyone involved would never forget the events that had taken place and years later it remains something I think back to.

It's fair to say that, friend or foe, colleague or complete stranger, the drive to save life is fundamental to humanity. I have no doubt that the terrorist incidents over recent years have been made all the more abhorrent because of the apparent devaluing of life – it's totally incomprehensible and perhaps explains the utter shock and disbelief when these attacks happen. How can anyone take the life of innocent people for absolutely no reason when we are hardwired to save life?

Throughout my career I have from time to time been able to help save lives. It's the greatest achievement, not because it is sometimes recognised through awards or accolades but because it has changed the course of so many lives for the better and that is the greatest reward of all.

I remember being on patrol and seeing the recovered victim of the stabbing walking with his family – that's the reward, that's the moment of reflection, that's one of the proudest things I've ever done. Ask any cop, paramedic, firefighter, doctor or nurse and they will all say the same – it's about the people.

A retired colleague and dear friend of mine, Ben, has told me the tale of saving the life of a child while on holiday in Egypt. He saw the boy face down in the swimming pool and lifeless, and he just sensed that something was not right. It definitely wasn't right: the boy wasn't breathing. So Ben carried him to the side of the pool and, while others stood around and watched, he started CPR.

The young boy, who was Russian, was rushed to hospital with his life hanging in the balance and my friend and his own family then got on their plane and flew back to the UK. That young boy survived due to the actions of a complete stranger in a foreign land who had done his best. There is a family on the other side of the world today who will be forever indebted and grateful to Ben, and it also shows that saving lives should have no boundaries – race, religion or nationality have no bearing at all.

It never ceases to amaze me to what lengths members of the public will go to save a life. Whether it is dragging someone off a train track, pulling someone from a burning car, wading into freezing water to rescue someone or tackling armed terrorists, the will to save life is both heroic and truly humbling. So, if you are ever unfortunate enough to be in that position, just do your best. It's better to try and fail than to not have tried at all. But most of all, take care of yourself – you only get one life.

12

Black Friday

FOR ANY COPS out there, Black Friday is a day to avoid at all costs. It is the Friday in the run up to Christmas that is earmarked as the 'big one', the one where most people will be knocking off work and starting their festive break. Sounds nice enough – almost peaceful – but the reality is often very different with unprecedented demand and calls for service. Unlike its recently coined namesake, it has nothing to do with shopping or people storming supermarkets and electrical stores to get the best deals in the run up to Christmas. It is normally a fairly obvious date and I, for one, would check our duty rosters to see if we had the misfortune of working it.

On Friday 16 December, 2011, it was our turn and we knew it would be a challenging night. We briefed just before 5 p.m. and had eleven hours of pure response policing ahead of us.

I sometimes felt that these nights were actually very straightforward – there would be no time for outstanding workloads to be progressed or that statement that we'd been trying to get or CCTV to review. It would be emergency call after emergency call and we'd be living in the moment and trying to hold the line.

As the sergeant, the biggest challenge, as always, was the resourcing of all these incidents. There is a finite number of officers on duty and it would probably surprise the public to know how few that is, but we punched well above our weight and our team was sound, really sound.

The briefing set the tone for the night and we all agreed that we needed to get out there, look after each other and work hard. I remember leaving the briefing room and there was a real sense of excitement tinged with apprehension. It's the sort of vibe you get at the start of a New Year's Eve late shift and it's the sort of shift that good officers revel in.

It didn't take long to take off and, predictably, after a short initial period of calm, it gained pace.

The first major incident that I attended was the most tragic of situations and epitomised just how unpredictable our work is. It had nothing to do with the increased number of people out and about celebrating the Christmas holidays; it was a desperately sad loss of life.

A call came in that there had been an industrial accident at Ipswich docks and that two people had been crushed under some metal pontoons that were being unloaded from a lorry. It was the type of incident that deserved the highest priority and within a few minutes all of the emergency services were in attendance.

It became clear very quickly what had happened – a lorry had arrived at the docks and was in the process of lifting the pontoons off the back using a hydraulic crane, which was affixed to the vehicle. As one of the pontoons was lifted, the lorry tipped and the remaining pontoons slid off the back and crushed two workers, one fatally. The stabilising legs had not been put out and this meant that the weight of the pontoon literally pulled the lorry over.

The scene was one of frantic activity, with paramedics treating the injured man. The police have a key role to play in saving life and during these incidents it is all hands to the pump, but we would also have the added dimension of considering the investigation. This is vital as the family of the deceased man would want to understand what had happened, why it had happened and perhaps who was ultimately responsible for the death of their loved one. As coroners sometimes explain to the jury and others present, an inquest is a fact-finding enquiry to ascertain the circumstances of the person's death. This can mean so much to the family, and so helping any future inquest is something that officers must consider during the initial running around.

My attention also turned to notifying the family of the man who had died. It is one of the hardest parts of the job and there is no easy way of giving someone that news. Cops frequently refer to them as 'agony' messages, but perhaps the significance of the word is lost: it truly is agony for the family and friends.

I would carefully consider who to send to issue an agony message – are they the right person for the job and will they be able to cope with the pressure? Some may say that's ridiculous, all cops should be able to give that news to anyone, but for me this is the most important job and it may be the only time we would ever have contact with that family, so it has to be done absolutely right.

I've delivered hundreds of agony messages and it was often true that, after the first few words, or sometimes before I even opened my mouth, the person wouldn't really take a great deal in, but every situation is different and police officers need to be ready.

I remember one situation where I had to tell an elderly lady that her husband had died in the town centre and she just hugged me and wouldn't, couldn't let go. Her world had just fallen apart and she just needed some common humanity, someone to hold and someone to be strong and silent for her.

If any police officer says this doesn't affect them, they are lying or they're in the wrong job.

The incident on the docks lasted for many hours, with crime scene investigators, CID and a number of people from the port itself all attending. I recall it being a miserable, wet, windy night and this reflected the sombre mood.

The shift continued to gather pace and, as expected, resources were becoming stretched. It was like a game of Top Trumps – what job was the most important and which would just have to wait.

At around 10 p.m. I went with another sergeant to arrest a lad for an urgent prison recall. This means that a person has been released from prison but they remain on licence and they are being recalled due to breaching the terms of their release. This can be for a variety of reasons, perhaps bad behaviour or failing to comply with a residency condition or curfew.

We decided that we'd get the arrest made before we then turned our attention to the pubs and clubs in town. We arrived at the address and located the man – he was no problem and we were soon off to custody.

I decided to whizz round the bypass so I was making my way through a local housing estate when the control room requested units for an explosion. I turned to my colleague and said, 'Did they just say explosion?' He confirmed that they had.

It's not often that I'd get called to explosions and what's more, we were so close that we were already turning into the road. I turned to my right and could immediately see that we had a big problem.

A flat above a shop had exploded and there was debris everywhere, while a burglar alarm from a nearby shop was sounding. It was reminiscent of the scenes you see on television where terrorist bombs have exploded and there is glass, brick, rubble and metal strewn across the street.

I stopped the car and told my colleague that I'd go and see what had happened while he waited with the detainee. I ran over the road and could see that someone had put up a ladder to the canopy above the shopfront which would then allow access to the first-floor flat.

A man from across the road shouted, 'Oi copper, I think that there's someone in there!'

I decided that I needed to get up there and, seeing that the police had arrived, the members of the public stepped aside and up I went. Another man followed me up and we approached the flat.

The windows were completely missing and there was the glint of smashed glass everywhere. I remember frantically sniffing the air but there was no smell of gas. That was a relief but it was far from an ideal way to enter the flat.

I got to the window and with my torch I could see a man crumpled in the corner of the front room, black and smouldering and clearly in shock. There was no more time to worry about the smell of gas. This man needed help, now.

I climbed in through the window and the force and devastation of the explosion was clear to see. There were bricks embedded in the walls, in the ceiling and in the floor. The room was not on fire, but there was a thin black film of soot and ash that covered everything, even the man in the corner. A thick fog of smoke hung in the air, meaning that it was hard to catch my breath.

We began to provide first aid to the man but it was as though he felt no pain – he was trying to move his legs but they just concertinaed up in front of his very eyes as though there wasn't a single bone left intact.

'Just try and stay nice and still,' I said to him. 'You're going to be OK – the ambulance is on the way.'

His eyes were bright in comparison to his blackened and bloodied face. How could anyone survive these injuries? It was as though he was conscious and awake, but his mind was in complete shock. His responses were slow and incoherent.

It was also clear that he was still smouldering, with smoke coming from his clothes and body. The man who had come into the flat with me crouched next to me as we tried to reassure the victim.

'Go and get some water,' I instructed. The man came back with a bowl of water so we could try and soothe the burns. I poured the water on his bare, blackened legs and to my astonishment it turned to steam. I'll never forget the sound and smell as the water evaporated in front of us.

We continued to reassure the man, encouraging him to stay strong. 'You're doing really well, stay with us.'

After what seemed like a few minutes the fire service arrived and approached the front door of the flat, which we'd now opened. A paramedic was stood by the front door and asked the firefighters if it was safe to enter.

The fire officer turned to me and asked, 'Can you smell gas inside?'

'No, definitely not. But we really need some help in here now.'

The flat then became a hive of activity with paramedics and firefighters working tirelessly to stabilise the man and evacuate him from the flat. It was a bizarre situation, one that was completely unexpected and once again we were thrown into the midst of trying to save a life.

The paramedics managed to stabilise the lad and get him to hospital. As he left the flat, I was almost certain that he would not survive and it would turn into a fatality. As a police officer you are not qualified in a lot, but you become experienced in almost everything and, in my opinion, the burns looked serious and the injuries catastrophic so I was not hopeful.

When I came outside the street was full of members of the public, some residents from nearby flats and houses, and a number of people from the pub opposite. They had heard the explosion and had come running out to see what had happened so they too were confronted by the scene of utter devastation.

It was one of those incidents where everyone was on the same side – someone got the ladder, others called 999 and everyone was willing on the emergency services. These non-crime-related incidents really do bring out the best in human nature and community spirit – even when some of them have had a bit too much to drink!

I returned to my police car, which was still parked up by the bus stop opposite, and I was relieved to see that my colleague and our prisoner were no longer sat waiting. Another police unit had picked them up. I can only begin to imagine what they had been thinking when they suddenly found themselves sat with a front-row seat. It would have been a great story for the guy to tell his mates when he got to jail, though.

It turned out that two other occupants of the flat had had a lucky escape. They were late home and as a result they were not inside at the time of the explosion. It turned out that the explosion had actually been caused by a redundant back boiler – it had heated up and then gone off like a bomb. Remarkably, the man from the flat survived and, what's more, he has made a decent recovery. He underwent multiple operations and spent months in hospital, but through the expert care and treatment he received from the wonderful NHS, he lives to fight another day. I was delighted to hear my initial assessment was wrong.

As with all shifts like this, they just keep going and this was no exception. A young man died in Felixstowe following an incident in which he was stabbed, there was a fatal road traffic collision, and this was over and above the usual drunken fights and public disorder linked to the pubs and clubs. It was hard to believe that this was the unofficial start of the Christmas holidays as it didn't feel very festive. It was a good example of always having to expect the unexpected.

13

I'm glad he's OK

YOU'VE ALL SEEN movies in which there is an armed siege and the SWAT team arrive, supported by hostage negotiators. It all looks very glamorous and I'd be lying if I said I didn't get a buzz out of it. But I think the magnitude of what is being done is sometimes lost in the hustle and bustle of operational incidents like this. Negotiators are there to try and prevent harm and ultimately save people's lives. That is what really appealed to me when I decided to apply to become a negotiator. It was taking me back to the very essence of why I joined the police; I wanted to help people and keep them safe irrespective of who they were. It is also a 'tactical option' that can resolve situations without any use of force at all. The British police are world renowned for their policing model, which is based on policing by consent – the police are the public and the public are the police.

It's fair to say that the negotiators' course was the most brutal and draining experience I've had within the police. Long, long days of over fifteen hours, which tested our mental agility and our communication skills to the max.

The days would start with several hours in the classroom and they would culminate with role playing to put it all into practice. The realism of the scenarios was fantastic and the pressure we all felt as we were constantly being assessed certainly made it a good test to see if we could handle such situations in real life. It also prepared us for how long these incidents can take – very rarely would they be resolved quickly and, despite what people may think, that was absolutely no failing on the part of the negotiators.

The course also taught us that by becoming a negotiator you are joining a family who all understand the demands and the pressures of the role. We all had a genuine desire to help people and were there to look after each other as well.

One of the training team was a man called Win Bernard. He is without doubt one of the most inspirational people I have ever met. He made negotiating sound so simple and he had an ability to hold the attention of a room so that all of us were hanging on to every word he said. He was the sort of guy that you wanted to bump into and chat to at every opportunity.

As someone who has watched and coached sport at a very high level, I am always amazed at how easy elite athletes make it look; I think that Win was the same but in this case it was negotiating – he was the best of the best. At the end of my Regional Negotiators' Course he reduced the entire room to tears with his speech. A great, great man.

Having completed the course I then became a qualified hostage and crisis negotiator and a part of our twenty-four-hour-a-day on-call rota. This meant that during periods of being on call I'd have a rucksack with me at all times, filled with kit, food and warm clothes, and I'd be ready to be deployed at a moment's notice irrespective of when that may be.

You may be thinking that it seems a bit extreme to have a full-time cadre of negotiators waiting for the call. You may also be thinking that there surely aren't that many armed sieges in Suffolk. You'd be right on the second point, for sure. However, something I learnt very quickly was just how often we'd be called out to people who were in crisis and considering taking their own life.

It is a desperately sad reality that people can find themselves hitting rock bottom; the reasons will be unique to that individual but the outcome is the same – they have given up hope that life can get better and they are on the verge of making the ultimate decision.

I'm embarrassed to say that as a society there seems to be a lack of compassion for people in these situations. How often have you been delayed or affected by someone who has shut a bridge or railway line because they are threatening to kill themselves? In my experience the frustration of being delayed seems to eclipse any concern or compassion for the person involved.

I remember being on a train to Edinburgh and, about ten minutes from Waverley station, the train suddenly ground to a halt. After a few moments an announcement came over the Tannoy that there was 'an incident' at the station and there would be a further update in due course. After a few minutes the frustration of people in the carriage grew and grew. 'What the hell is going on?'

Then another passenger joined in, 'Oh, for God's sake.' I sat there, quietly listening and thinking about what it was likely to be. I thought either someone had been hit by a train or someone was threatening to take their own life. Perhaps that is a sign of what we do as police officers – we generally fear the worst! I hoped the person was OK.

After around fifteen minutes the Tannoy crackled into life again and the announcement was made that we'd not be moving until further notice. Another passenger then received a text message from a relative who was at the station waiting for their arrival. It informed them that someone had climbed onto a ledge and was threatening to kill themselves and the police were talking to him. The passenger relayed that information to the carriage and was met with a chorus of dissatisfaction. The passenger opposite me said, 'Selfish bastard.'

I remember thinking, *What the fuck are you talking about? Someone has reached a point so low, so dark and so desperate that they are thinking of taking their life, and that is being selfish because you're stuck on a train with half a glass of wine and a packet of crisps? No, it's definitely not selfish.*

I contemplated having a word with the moron and making my point but, in truth, I was so angry I'd have probably ended up getting myself into trouble. It did, however, make me think just how determined I was to be a negotiator and to help people.

I've often been asked, 'What do you say when you get there?' It's tricky because it's probably the hardest part of any conversation – getting started. Within the negotiator world it would be referred to as an 'opening line' and it would sometimes be debated at great length before deploying to the scene.

It would be something that we'd often practise with a colleague. 'Nah, that sounds crap, don't say that!' Some people may wonder why it's so important. It's because first impressions count and in this line of work it can be the difference between life and death.

I'd generally keep it simple, trying to make a connection with the person. 'Hello, my name is Ali. I'd really like to help.' It was always sincere and genuine; I really did want to help.

I remember when Dr Kate Granger MBE launched the 'Hello, my name is' campaign. Kate was terminally ill with cancer and she noticed how often the people providing her care did not introduce themselves. At the time the campaign was launched, Kate explained, 'I firmly believe it is not just about common courtesy, but it runs much deeper. Introductions are about making a human connection between one human being who is suffering and vulnerable, and another human being who wishes to help.' I couldn't agree with Kate more.

The type of incidents I attended were wide and varied but the common theme was that the people were in crisis. I recall one incident on the Orwell Bridge near Ipswich. I was called out at 3 a.m. on a freezing winter's night. I remember taking the call and being told the brief circumstances as I chucked on some clothes and grabbed my bag of kit. I then jumped in my car and within a few minutes I had arrived at the back of a small queue of traffic on the dual carriageway. I dumped my car on the side of the road and began to walk to the top of the bridge. I walked between the cars and, as I got to the highest point, I could see that there was a man sat on the parapet with his back to the drop. He seemed in a very precarious position and, as someone who doesn't like heights at the best of times, it made my blood run cold.

As I got a bit closer, I could see that two officers from the Armed Response Vehicle were talking to the man. They were calmly asking him to get down and from my perspective they were doing a really good job; their tone was calm and supportive and they were being genuine and kind.

After a few minutes I walked forward and the ARV boys explained who I was and I took over the negotiations. I use the term negotiations, but in truth I was there to listen and to talk. Negotiations have all sorts of connotations; you negotiate the sale of a house or the purchase of a car; you may negotiate a new contract at work. This seemed a little more sincere and less clinical than those everyday transactions, which can be lacking in any emotion or compassion. I remember this guy was really quite difficult to talk to; he was quiet and although the thoughts that were racing through his mind were written all over his face, he didn't seem to want to tell me about them.

As a negotiator you've got to do your best, be patient and persevere. After around an hour we'd barely spoken but he'd told me that he was struggling with a gambling addiction and he felt that he was better off dead. 'I've blown it all again. It was my last chance, I just can't take it any more.' He was a local man and he was definitely not the first person I'd spoken to about gambling addictions and the effect it had on their lives and their family's lives. 'They'd be much better off without me; they must be ashamed of me.'

'No, they won't be better off without you. It will change their lives for ever.' I remember thinking how surreal it was that here he was, in the early hours of the morning contemplating taking his own life, and here I was as the person charged with the responsibility of trying to save him. At any moment he could lean back and he'd be gone, his life extinguished.

I would always worry when people stopped talking at all as it could be that they were so focused on their thoughts that they were becoming disengaged. I was starting to fear the worst, so I thought it was time for me to do a bit more talking. I take you back to my comment about negotiations: this wasn't to close a deal or get a better price, I was now saying all that I could to save his life knowing that these could be the last words he ever heard. 'I think that things can and will get better,' I remember saying to him. 'Don't do it today. You can come back and do it tomorrow if you want to.' Some people reading this will be stunned by that comment. Negotiators save lives, it's what they do. If that man makes the decision right here, right now, there is no coming back, there is no second chance. It's the ultimate final act. He could do it in the future if he feels that is what he wants to do, but don't make that decision now. It is giving that person hope, the chance to back out of making that decision at that moment, taking the pressure off. And at these most desperate of times as a negotiator I had to try anything to save the person's life. During the time I was a negotiator I had never experienced any mental illness so I could only ever imagine how distressing it must have been.

People often think that negotiators are only there because they're getting paid and 'it's their job'. It was part of my job but I didn't have to be a negotiator, or get up at 3 a.m. in the middle of the night to talk to a complete stranger. I did it because I genuinely cared and I know that I speak for all negotiators when I say that.

After around an hour, quite unexpectedly he got down off the parapet and I walked over, took him by the hand and put my arm round his shoulder. 'You're OK, you're going to be OK.' He was upset and silently crying but he was alive.

He sat in the back of the traffic car. 'What is going to happen now?'

'We're going to take you up to the hospital to get you some help.' He desperately needed it.

Very rarely did I ever see the people again or find out what happened but I always left the scene with a great sense of worth and wishing them well. As I walked back through the line of traffic, the engines began to start, the headlights came back on and the drivers refastened their seatbelts. As I passed a lorry, the window was open and the driver leant out and said, 'Good job, buddy, I'm glad he's OK.' Now that is what it is about. Maybe he could have a word with the guy in the train carriage on the way to Edinburgh.

Sticking with the railway theme, I was the unfortunate negotiator who was deployed to Ipswich railway station in the summer of 2013 for a guy who had got on the roof. I remember it well as it was the start of the Latitude festival so the station was busy with eager festival goers. Unfortunately, the guy on the roof meant that no trains could operate out of the station as the power lines had been switched off so it was a high priority for a lot of people that this didn't go on for too long.

As a negotiator I didn't care how long it went on for; my job was to save life and if that took ten minutes, ten hours or even ten days it was not important. I began to negotiate but we were presented with a number of problems. First, the lad didn't speak English and I didn't speak Lithuanian. Second, we were constantly being heckled by members of the public from a nearby block of flats. And third, it was hot. I had also just got back from Ireland where I'd suffered with severe sunburn so several hours in the sun was not really a good idea.

After a few hours perched on a ladder, we managed to get a cherry picker from a local firm. I'd never been in a cherry picker but it looked better than the ladder we had been using. We worked out that we could fit four of us in; the lad who'd operate the cherry picker, the interpreter and two negotiators. As he attempted to lift the platform an alarm sounded. He turned to me and said, 'It's too heavy.' We decided that he would have to tell me how to operate it and he'd have to get out. He also reassured me that if it all went wrong he could press a button and we'd all descend back to safety. Result. I then put my newfound skills as a crane operative into action. The same alarm sounded;

we were still too heavy. Well, the one person who definitely had to stay in was the interpreter, otherwise the game of charades that I'd been playing for the last three hours would continue. So the decision was made, it was me and the interpreter going up, so I'd have to drive and negotiate. I can assure you that the next four hours of my life were not the best; I hate heights and, although perfectly safe, the cherry picker swayed and creaked in the breeze.

Eventually a team of officers had to go up there and get him down. People often ask me what the issue was and why had he gone up there. Despite talking to him for hours and hours and hours, I still have no idea. The main thing was that he lived to tell the tale.

It's hard to recall all of the incidents that I dealt with as a negotiator but over the years it was a lot. Of the people I spoke to, I think the overwhelming majority had the intention to take their life, or were certainly seriously considering it. I like to think that I played a small part in helping them and giving them that second chance. If any of them ever read this, I just want them to know that I meant every word I said to them; I do care, I do hope that they get the help that they need, and I do believe that things can and will get better. Take care.

14

Battered but not broken

WHEN PEOPLE JOIN the police I'm not sure if they ever really know what they are signing up for. I certainly didn't. Of course, I had a rough idea what the police did, and then, as I progressed through training, I began to get a feel for the diverse role that I was about to take on.

In addition to the emotional and mental scars that police officers pick up, they can also collect quite a few physical ones too. On the whole cops don't get seriously hurt, thank goodness, and I think that is testament to their tenacity and training. When I first started, the training involved standing in lines and hitting pads with our batons. Now the police train in a far more realistic way and, as they say, train hard and fight easy. It's true. I just wish that as assaults on officers go up, and the risk of terrorism prevails and complaints increase, we would stop reducing the frequency of the training. Sooner or later someone will get seriously hurt and then I suspect that there will be a sea change but it will be too little too late for the cop who gets hurt and their family.

I had a bad run of injuries in the police. I attended a nightclub for a lad causing problems and, on my arrival, he was out the front, causing a scene and being generally abusive. Within a few minutes he had said enough and was going to be arrested, but as we moved in he legged it. He was a young lad, probably only late teens at the time, but I was fairly quick back in the day so off we went. I chased him across the road and away from the club. It was as though he suddenly had that sobering thought – he was drunk and hardly dressed for the occasion and now he was being chased by an officer who he knew well and, what's more, who he knew would be too quick for him. He put up the best effort he had but within about 25 metres I was with him and tackled him to the ground.

Unfortunately, as we went to the floor my right foot caught on the kerb and there was an almighty crack and then searing pain. I had hold of the lad and I had no intention of letting go, but I'll be honest, I was desperately hoping that the cavalry was about to arrive. They did, and as they took control of the offender I was able to roll away and then try and lift myself up using the fence as a crutch. I was pretty sure that I had broken something as it felt as though my foot had folded up the wrong way inside my boot. During the ride to hospital on the back seat of the police car, I was not really looking forward to them taking my boot off.

The one thing you can rely on in these situations is a lot of attention – not the supportive, caring sort but the piss-taking type, so when I did get wheeled into Accident and Emergency there was already a gaggle of colleagues there to meet me. I started to think about the practicalities of my boot being taken off. The colleague who had driven me up to the hospital offered his opinion, 'That is going to really hurt!' Thanks for that! The X-rays came back and I had snapped my foot, all four bones right across the middle, and one of them had broken twice.

Before I knew it I was wearing a protective cast and learning how to use crutches. It was a setback but I am the sort of person who always wants to contribute so, having had the cast fitted, I headed back to work to finish my shift. The other thing that I am is very, very impatient and when it comes to being restricted through injuries, there really is nothing worse. I remember being asked if I'd help out on the drugs team while I was injured as they had some big cases on the go and could do with an extra pair of hands to help with the paperwork. It sounded like a really good role, until I realised it was on the fourth floor of Ipswich nick and the lift only went to the third! I used to have to hop up the twenty-four steps each morning to get to the office. People also became accustomed to seeing me in the queue in the canteen on a wheelie office chair.

I hobbled around on crutches for six weeks and then went to Flint House, which is a Police Rehabilitation Centre. It is absolutely brilliant and provided me with top-class physio and rehab. My physio would see me every morning for some treatment and then I'd be off to the hydrotherapy pool or gym to work on my strength and balance. Some cops almost seem to go to Flint House for an annual holiday but that was not true in my case – it was a working holiday and a pretty painful one! It did mean, however, that having arrived barely able to walk, I left ten days later and went straight back to Ipswich to work a late shift on the Friday night.

Once, when I was just arriving for work and walked through the rear gates of Ipswich nick, a police car was just setting off on a shout. I asked what was going on and they told me it was a burglary in progress just around the corner. I jumped in the back of the car as, although I had no kit with me, I wanted to help if I could. We arrived within the blink of an eye – the premises was literally just across the road. I'd not normally have jumped in, but the last thing I wanted was for my colleague to arrive on his own and then be confronted by a burglar determined to escape and with his back-up still several minutes away. As we got to the business premises the burglar suddenly came out the back and over the rear wall. We were off! It was one of the few occasions when I didn't have the disadvantage of the body armour and kit that we have to carry so I felt that I was in with a good chance. I chased the lad down the road, over a park, past the football ground and then towards the river.

As we headed that way I was a little perplexed as to where he thought he was going – little did I know he planned to jump straight in the water. As he went to get over the river wall, I grabbed him and we began to struggle. I had hold of him but his bodyweight was over the other side and, for those of you who have ever seen *Cliffhanger*, it was a bit like the opening scene with my hand slipping from his. Unfortunately, my finger got caught in his glove and as he fell it snapped and dislocated. Now that hurt! To add insult to injury the driver of the police car then finally caught up with us, leant over the wall and nicked him.

Once I got to hospital the trauma was far from over. The staff nurse came over and explained, 'We've had a look at your X-ray and your finger has dislocated and the top part has twisted round the wrong way. We need to put that back in place.' He then asked if I would mind if the junior doctor who was with him carried out the procedure. It was a short conversation: yes, I would mind.

'No offence, mate, but I'd rather this guy did it!' I wanted the staff nurse to do it as he looked like he probably did five of these a day. Although I'm all up for a bit of practice and helping people learn, just not today and just not on my finger. The staff nurse and junior doctor were absolutely fine with that so we agreed that the nurse would do it. I was taken to a side room and sat in a chair for them to get to work.

Now, despite having been exposed to some of the goriest scenes you could ever imagine, I am not great with needles. The nurse explained to me what would happen. 'We'll give you an anaesthetic and then I'll put your finger back in place. It won't hurt, you'll just feel me pulling your finger a bit.' I sat back in the chair and the nurse advised that if I was not great with needles I ought to look away as he was going to anaesthetise my finger.

It was really sound advice, but, unfortunately, as he was tutoring the doctor, he began to describe in graphic detail what he was doing, 'So you put the first needle in the webbing of the finger and then when you feel it touch the bone . . .'

That was enough for me and the next thing I remember was a very worried-sounding junior doctor saying, 'Do you think we should get some help in here?' and a slightly worried nurse saying, 'Give him a minute, I'm sure he'll come back round.' The bonus was that while I was knocked out they had managed to yank my finger back into position, so every cloud and all that.

Other injuries have included a broken arm trying to smash the window of a car while the lad inside was trying to conceal drugs and money down his pants, and a cut eye from being punched in the face. The punch in the eye was a little bitter-sweet. I nicked a lad on the Cornhill in Ipswich – it's the main square in the centre of the town. I had been on the lookout for a lad who was wanted on a prison recall. He was a pretty difficult person to deal with and I suspected that he'd probably try and give us the slip. He was a small, athletic man who would probably be too quick for me.

As I drove through the town with a colleague, I spotted him

along with two other lads. It was late evening and the town centre was deserted. They were sat on some benches chatting. It was time to think on my feet. I told my colleague what was going on and that we'd try and play it cool and then grab him. The other two boys were on BMX bikes, so that would be my way in. I pulled up, opening the window of the police car. 'All right boys, how are you?'

'Yeah, all good thanks, officer,' replied one of the lads.

'What are you all up to? Just relaxing?' I asked.

'Yeah, yeah, yeah. Just chilling,' he said.

I started to get out of the car, 'We've had a report of some youngsters messing around on bikes. It's obviously not you as you're a bit older but have you seen anyone else on BMXs?' That was enough talking. I was now stood right next to him. I grabbed hold of him, 'You're nicked, stay calm.' Then it all went off – he began struggling and straining and spinning to get away. He managed to wriggle free so, before he got up and running, I made a last-ditch dive for him, rugby tackling him to the ground. I landed on top and, as he struggled to get away, he punched me straight in the face. All of a sudden my blood was dripping all over him from a cut above my eye, as I tried to pin him to the tarmac. I was starting to wonder where my colleague had gone as I seemed to be doing this solo.

It turned out that while he had been struggling with me, he had thrown a package of Class A drugs away and it was bouncing across the town square. We finally managed to get control and he subsequently went on trial at Norwich Crown Court. I was required to give evidence about the night in question. After a lengthy trial, mainly about his drug-dealing antics, the verdicts were delivered. He was found guilty of being a drug dealer and not guilty of punching me in the face! I respected the jury's decision but I could not believe it. He had managed to convince them that I had banged my head on the floor and that he had not punched me at all. I guess the silver lining to this cloud was that he got seven-and-a-half years for the drugs offences.

In the grand scheme of things these are all quite minor injuries but it's a risky job and if you are out there jumping over fences, driving fast and getting in fights with criminals determined to get away, you will get hurt. It also became apparent just how vulnerable we were to the mental torment of dealing with such difficult incidents.

I remember, when I first joined, I had friends who were joining the military and I reminisce now about how I considered some of the horrific things that they would see at war. Having been a police officer for many years I have seen those things as well and perhaps, unlike the military, we more frequently and intimately see the families and friends that are torn apart when tragedy strikes. I think all police officers would agree that the horror and gore is the easier part and it's the emotional torment that we witness that is sometimes too much to bear.

When I went through training, I was in the fortunate position that, as a young eighteen-year-old, I had never seen a dead body. So one of my concerns was whether I would be able to cope with it. While working at my first station, within days of starting we were called to attend a nursing home where an elderly resident had sadly passed away in their sleep. My heart began to pound and my mind began to race at the prospect of seeing someone who had died. When we got there the staff were lovely, really nice, in fact, and I guess they could tell that I was new to all of this, so we took it nice and slowly as we worked through the paperwork and called the Coroner's Ambulance.

Little did I know that, as time went on, and certainly having worked in Ipswich for fifteen years, sometimes barely a day would go past without me dealing with death. It gives you real perspective to your own life and it makes me grateful to be healthy and for my family to be healthy.

My first truly traumatic incident, over and above normal business, was to deal with an incident on the Orwell Bridge. We attended the bridge in the middle of the night, initially as a result of a car being seen abandoned on the carriageway. This is a notorious area for people to kill themselves so we were fairly sure that someone had probably jumped as there was nobody with the car and nobody walking along the road.

We got out of the police car and, using a large torch, we peered over the parapet. It's only when you actually stop on the bridge that you suddenly realise just how high it is; the wind whistles across it even on a calm day and it makes you feel pretty vulnerable. As we looked over we could see a body lying on the concrete footings below. All of a sudden, though, just at the edge of the torch light, we spotted something else.

As we moved the torch this second object looked like a giant laying there and then we realised – the first body we could see was a child and the second was a man (his father). It was incomprehensible. How had a child been thrown or fallen from the bridge? As the night wore on the coastguard teams recovered the bodies and brought them to the shore, where we met them. The little lad was still wearing his pyjamas. How could this have happened? How could anyone do this to their own child? Just why? When officers attended the home address, they found that the wife had been murdered. It was the most horrific of situations and it made me realise that life is sometimes so wrong, so messed up and so inexplicable, and yet we have to deal with it, somehow.

I went to the hospital with the two bodies and as we walked into the mortuary the enormity of it hit me – this little boy's life had been extinguished and he now lay in a hospital morgue surrounded by adults and generally older people who had lived their lives. It was just not fair. I remember how deeply affected I was as a result of this, but somehow I just moved on from it.

I also had the misfortune of dealing with a fire in which two young children died. I arrived on scene as the fire engines came down the road but it was clear to all of us we were just too late. The family came running towards the blue lights and sirens, screaming that their children were still inside and pleading for help, but in their heart of hearts, they too knew we could do nothing to save them. It is the strangest feeling knowing that the ground on which you're stood is so close and yet you are literally in a different world to the person who has lost their life. I stood, watching the flames destroy the property and no amount of noise or commotion seemed to break my stare. This is where the role of a police officer is so different to so many others.

We had to begin the awful task of recovering the two bodies and trying to comfort the family. You can't comfort the family, really, as there is nothing you can say, nothing you can do, nothing at all. I would tell new officers not to try to do too much, just be there, be strong, be silent, be solemn, be professional and most of all be kind and be compassionate. I had to attend the hospital with the bodies and hand them over to the mortuary staff. It was horrific and it affected me deeply but within minutes of leaving the hospital I was required to attend another incident, and another, and another.

I guess over the years I had learnt to deal with these events by simply moving on – it makes them sound insignificant but it certainly isn't meant to. Some may think that to continually move on is just burying my head in the sand, and to some degree I guess that could be argued, but the level and frequency of tragedy are sometimes so high that to dwell on each and every incident would be impossible. We all deal with tragedy differently. Some would also argue that perhaps you're storing all these events up and one day they will all come crashing down around you, but almost twenty years in it seemed to be working for me, more or less.

When tragedy did strike at work, it certainly made me feel that I was living and working in two different worlds, almost two different lives. That is not just when dealing with trauma, but also with crime and some of the most abhorrent individuals you could possibly imagine. Most cops, like most other professionals, will live a nice life – have a nice house, drive a nice car, have a nice family and have nice friends. They will go to nice places and do nice things. And then they come to work and they go to some of the worst houses you can imagine and deal with some of the most dysfunctional situations. I guess that is why cops generally don't live and work in the same area as, for their own sanity, they try and keep these lives separate.

I would also echo the views of others when they say that having worked in a place for a long time, you can't drive anywhere without recalling particular incidents or events. Some of them are happy occasions, though: a certain street where we had a really good arrest or dealt with a really decent person, or somewhere that something funny happened.

On the whole, though, it is the more serious incidents that leave their mark all over the town. The incident on the roof of the car park had a huge effect on me and every day when I drive past that car park I will glance up at the ledge and remember what happened. I may drive past several times a day, but it will still act as a reminder. There's also a particular house where we dealt with the death of a young child and I cannot drive down that road without thinking of the poor lad and his family. I am not very religious but I will say a prayer as I pass and hope that they are doing OK. And it reminds me of a quote that I heard, 'No matter how good or bad your life is, wake up each morning and be thankful that you still have one.' I am very thankful.

15

That's it, you're nicked

IN 2010, I was quietly going about my business as a response sergeant in Ipswich when I received a call from our press office. I had been aware that there had been a Freedom of Information request in relation to identifying the top arresting officers in the UK and much to my surprise I was top.

I had been completing some public order training in a place not far from Ipswich so when I was summoned back to the police station, as there were several reporters there to see me, it all became a bit surreal.

The crux of it was that I had been identified as the top arresting officer with 524 arrests in the previous twelve months. I had never really paid too much attention to my arrest figures and, being an officer who had only ever worked in Ipswich, I had no idea whether that was high or not compared to colleagues elsewhere in the UK. When I got back to the nick, there were at least five or six journalists who wanted to speak to me and it's fair to say the next few days were bizarre.

On the day that the news broke I was even whisked down to London so I could appear on *GMTV* the following morning to be interviewed. Apparently, most cops make on average fewer than ten arrests a year and yet I had made over five hundred. I knew that would generate an awful lot of interest but also a whole lot of scrutiny. Who were all these people? Had any of them actually done anything wrong? How many of them actually went to court and were convicted? What are all the other cops doing? I had my views on all of these things and so too would other people.

Making arrests is a fundamental part of being a police officer, but there is much more to policing than that. Those people who know me and know my arrest record may think that is a curious thing for me to say but it's absolutely right. The work of a police officer and the police force as a whole is diverse, complex and multifaceted, but at some point, people who are committing offences will need to be brought to justice and often this will mean being arrested.

Right from a young age, parents tell their overexcited mischievous children, 'Be good or the policeman will take you away,' and children play games of cops and robbers in the playground. I really wish that parents wouldn't tell their children that the policeman will take them away, or at least not with such gusto and sinister tones, as it's important that when their child really does need the police, they are not scared senseless at the prospect of being taken away and locked up. Ironically, however, with older teenagers, it would be quite nice if the parents did occasionally warn their children that their actions do come with consequences!

It's also interesting to hear the expressions used for making an arrest, 'Go home now or you're going to get locked up,' or 'That's it, you're nicked.' These words are said by cops up and down the country hundreds, in fact thousands, of times a day, perhaps often with little recognition of just how significant an action it is. To arrest someone is to take away their liberty, something which everyone is entitled to and something that in a modern civilised society is a core human right. Having said that, we'd all agree that where there is good justification, arresting someone is appropriate and fundamental to keeping society civil.

My arrests that year had actually been fairly low when I looked into it. Some years I had made almost seven hundred arrests and in the first fifteen years of my career I made almost five thousand. That's a lot of arrests and with that comes a huge amount of work. Detaining people also comes with a lot of risk. Fortunately, most people are compliant but that wasn't really my area of business: I was heavily involved in policing the nightlife in Ipswich where often people would be drunk and lively, and also I was dealing with our most prolific offenders. Contrary to popular belief, I wasn't arresting petty criminals for minor offences all day long just to get my numbers up! And because I had always been seen as a busy officer who did make a lot of arrests I felt the glare of scrutiny more than most, so when deciding on whether to lock someone up or not that was an added consideration. I'm sure that resulted in an awful lot of people being given the benefit of the doubt.

After my arrest figures were thrust into the public glare, I got a lot of criticism about doing the job of a PC and not a sergeant. I remember thinking, *What a lot of nonsense!* I had not got promoted to do less work, I had got promoted to work hard and make as big a contribution as I possibly could – all for the greater good. There are thousands of people out there committing crime every day, not to mention the lists of people who are wanted by the police. There is no quota or limit, and the work of the police will never, ever be done. A lot of my arrests were self-generated – drink drivers, drug dealers, people committing burglaries or going equipped to steal. I took my supervisory responsibilities very seriously and this was reflected in the outstanding results of the team; they were highly competent officers who didn't need a sergeant to hold their hand all day or to be micro-managed, so I would go out and add my firepower. My work ethic was always such that if there was any spare capacity then I'd find something to fill it and that's exactly what I did.

I also worked in some tough parts of town, the sort of places where if you left your police car unattended, when you returned it may have had no front windscreen, or all the tyres might have been slashed. It was in these types of environment that I had cut my teeth and honed my skills. I didn't trust anyone and as such wouldn't give an inch. A good example was one particular arrest outside a busy parade of shops. It was an infamous location having been subject to the first ever dispersal orders in Suffolk in 2003 and it could be an intimidating place to work. A colleague and I drove past the shops and I spotted a well-known lad who was wanted for a series of burglaries. He was a horrible individual who had no qualms about breaking into your house and ransacking it while you slept. The issue on this occasion was that he was with a group of around twenty of his mates and they all had potential. We spun round the block and came up with a plan. We'd get out and play it cool, and then when we were close enough, we'd get our hands on the burglar. Sounded simple!

We pulled up next to the group, got out and sauntered over, chatting inconspicuously. Once I was within arm's reach, I launched myself at him and grabbed hold of his hoody. Well, that was the easy bit. The group quickly surrounded us, erupting into hostility and grabbing hold of their friend and trying to wrestle him free. This was quite a common tactic in this part of town and if they could 'rescue' one of their own, it would be the greatest prize. It's at times like that when the disparity between training and reality was never clearer. I had no chance of handcuffing him because if I took one hand off to grab my cuffs then he'd be gone before I knew it. So, the predictable stand-off continued with me holding him against the shop window with all my might and my colleague trying to keep the baying crowd back.

Fortunately, after a minute or two I could hear sirens approaching from every direction: the cavalry arrived and the game was up. I became quite well known among my colleagues for just not letting go.

I do remember some arrests more than others and now I look back they seem almost bizarre. As my reputation grew among the criminal fraternity, I'd often get them calling me at work to see if they were wanted, or their solicitors would make enquiries on their behalf. I would also sometimes call them myself and see if we could do things the easy way as they really wouldn't want it to be the hard way; that normally involved being woken up at 5 a.m. and possibly needing to replace their damaged front door. It certainly wasn't unusual for them to arrange to meet me on a street corner to hand themselves in.

Over the years I arrested some dangerous people, some of the most dangerous people that you could imagine. Murderers, rapists, armed robbers, people with a propensity to cause the greatest harm with absolutely no regard for their victims. When these people are arrested, they often feel they haven't got a lot to lose so the risks are high. I'd always warn younger officers in service, be very wary of someone who thinks they've got nothing to lose because any control that they might have had is likely to be gone.

I specifically recall an incident involving a man I arrested on warrant. He was an athletic, muscular man and he had something about him that made me nervous. So nervous that when we located him hiding under a bed he was handcuffed immediately behind his back. We got him a jacket to put over his shoulders as I wasn't even comfortable with taking the cuffs off for him to get dressed.

When the handcuffs did eventually come off in the charge room of the custody suite, he knocked out a colleague of mine and broke his jaw. I have never felt so responsible and so sick as a result of seeing a colleague harmed to such an extent but this guy clearly felt he had nothing left to play for so he took his chance to inflict grievous injuries on a police officer. As soon as the blow was delivered, we leapt into action; I emptied a can of CS spray directly into his face and, as he knelt down to his haunches, another officer and I bundled him to the floor. The cuffs were back on and he was off to a cell, but the damage had already been done. It's incidents like this that drove me on during my career as it's violent criminals like him that are the ones society needs to be protected from.

A lot of people ask me, how did you do it? How could you arrest so many people? It sounds glib but it starts with working hard, really hard. Being a police officer is a strange role in many ways and contrary to what people may think when they're drunk and mouthing off in the back of a police van, no, cops don't get paid any more for arresting people. There are plenty of jobs in the private sector that incentivise good performance, but the police have no big bonuses or commission for their staff. It is a case of doing the right thing for the right reasons, and in my role working on the front line, often that did mean arresting people. I feel very strongly that police officers working in front-line roles, particularly on response teams, work as hard as anyone else I know. I was very fortunate that I worked in Ipswich for many years and with this continuity came a vast knowledge of local offenders. There are some criminals who I saw and spoke to more than my own family and friends, and not surprisingly we are on first name terms.

The more criminals you know, the more arrests you will make – it's amazing how many times I'd arrest someone whose name had been circulated as wanted and they would tell me that they had seen loads of cops but nobody had picked them up. The chances are the cops they had seen didn't know them and simply didn't recognise them. I was a real people watcher and I'd spend hours patrolling the streets in my police car, trying to take it all in. Who did I see associating with who? Where did I see them last? What were they wearing? What part of town do they normally frequent? It's all very relevant.

Knowing this many people also meant that I'd be contacted on a daily basis by officers and staff wanting to show me CCTV images of suspects in the hope that I may be able to identify them. I guess I am one of those people who rarely forgets a face and over the years you even start to recognise the way certain people walk and carry themselves. Maybe it's a strange gait, or a bounce, or a shuffle. Perhaps they hold their arms down to their side, or they swing them enthusiastically.

I remember some CCTV footage for an armed robbery that had happened just before we came on duty, and although he had gone to some effort to cover his face with a scarf, as soon as I saw the footage of the offender walking away from the camera I thought I knew who it was, and so it proved. We arrested him later that night and recovered the clothing he had been wearing and the gun. There were also plenty of occasions I'd not be able to identify people – the images may have been poor quality or the camera was just not in the right place. That was fine as well. I could only say what I thought.

Within the police I became known as someone who could find whoever you were looking for. Every single shift I'd receive requests from detectives on CID or local beat officers asking if I could keep an eye out for someone they needed to be arrested. It meant that most shifts I had a list of two or three suspects who we'd go out looking for in between attending emergencies and my supervisory responsibilities. Sometimes these requests were because the officer in charge of the investigation couldn't be bothered to do it themselves; sometimes it was because the suspect was difficult to track down; sometimes it was because they were particularly dangerous and needed an appropriate response; and sometimes some were more urgent than others.

I always liked the operational nature of my work. It meant that it was important to consider lots of different things: fitness, tactics, equipment, driving, local knowledge; they were all key components to be effective as a police officer and they all needed to be worked on and continually improved. I think that most people would agree that the fitness levels for operational officers are very low and to be effective you have to aim far, far higher. I always prided myself on being fit for purpose and if it came down to a foot chase, I'd back myself more often than not.

I was also able to think jobs through and I was able to put myself in the mind of the offender; where would I go, what route would I take, whose address would I hide out at? Over time I'd get to know how certain individuals or groups of offenders operated and that knowledge definitely gave me an advantage.

Sometimes colleagues seemed surprised at my knack of spotting when things weren't quite right. Some say it's a sixth sense, others would say it's professional judgement; whatever it is, it's vital if you are going to be prolific when it comes to making arrests. I would spend hours researching different parts of town so that I knew all the rat runs that might be used and I'd make sure that when travelling across Ipswich I'd know the fastest possible routes so I got there in double quick time.

You often hear police officers complimenting other officers for being a great 'thief taker', as it's not something that everyone can do. That doesn't mean that they don't contribute in other ways but, at some point, we do need to track these people down and lock them up.

One crucial element of my kind of policing was to be streetwise so that when opportunities presented themselves, they didn't go to waste. I worked with some amazing officers who had the ability to look completely relaxed no matter what the situation but underneath they were like a coiled spring ready to leap into action. They had covered off any escape routes, moved potential weapons out of arms reach and they would pick their moment perfectly. I worked hard on this as well as you had to always make sure you were one step ahead. Nothing was more satisfying than swooping on an unsuspecting suspect and, before they knew what was happening, they were safely in custody.

It was also important to get out there and see what you could find. Any town will have lists and lists of wanted people but I've never found any of them wandering around the nick or sitting in the report-writing room! Just driving from incident to incident I'd see and recognise known offenders and more often than not they'd be wanted. I also had the knack of recognising people I'd never met, having been shown a photograph or CCTV image. Lots of people ask me how I did that. I have no idea. I had just always been someone who could remember a face and I was good with names.

I recall one lad who was wanted for a series of burglaries in another part of the county but we had been informed that he might be staying in Ipswich. We all sat in a briefing and were shown the mugshot and given the details of the offences he was wanted for. Later that day, I drove through one of the housing estates and saw a guy sat at a bus stop. He had his hood up and his face was partially covered with a scarf. 'That's our man!' We spun the car round and after a short foot chase he was sat in the back of our car and off to custody.

Another example that springs to mind related to a house burglary. It's incredibly rare that police officers catch people in the act of committing a burglary, particularly house break-ins. We would regularly get called and nick people nearby but to get someone inside an address was gold dust and the stuff of legend.

I was working a pretty normal Saturday evening shift and came across a lad walking down the road with a kitchen knife stuck in his back. It was one of those moments when you do a double take! I said to my colleague, 'Has that lad got a knife stuck in his back?' We slowed down, took a closer look and, yes, he certainly did! You might be thinking, *I thought we were talking about house burglaries*. Bear with me! The blade of the kitchen knife was about 10 inches long and was sticking out of his shoulder blade. Despite this, he was not cooperative at all and although he was happy for the paramedics to take him to hospital, he certainly wasn't going to tell us what had happened.

I knew him well and I had my suspicions that it may have been as a result of a domestic so we attended his home address to see what was going on and, in all truth, nick his girlfriend.

When we got there I had a quick look into the front room through a gap in the curtains. Much to my amazement I could see two well-known burglars in the process of piling up all the valuables in the corner of the room. Incidentally, one of them was the guy responsible for breaking and dislocating my finger a few months earlier! They were giggling away to each other while holding their sleeves over their hands, presumably to avoid leaving any fingerprints. I could not believe my eyes. Not only had the victim been stabbed somehow, but now his house was being burgled as well. I turned to my colleague and frantically whispered for him to get round the back while calling up for more units to attend.

After a few minutes the team descended on the residential street and on the count of three we burst into the house. All hell broke loose as both suspects attempted to run. Unfortunately for them we were more than a couple of steps ahead and they were both nicked in the house.

When we searched the area we found their car just around the corner and it was full of computers and electrical items from a nearby business that had been screwed earlier in the evening. Result!

It just shows, though, that you never really know how these scenarios will end and you sometimes just have to go with the flow and see what happens. I would often tell colleagues, 'We don't write the scripts but we do write the endings,' and this typified that.

And sometimes you just need to be lucky. I was working a hot summer late shift and we had been made aware of an absconder from the local prison. He had been due to return to the jail the day before but he had not turned up and his name had been circulated as wanted. The team were aware and we had been given the description.

As part of our patrols I decided to drive through Christchurch Park; it is an amazing park and somewhere that attracts a lot of people so it's nice to drive through and fly the flag.

On our way through I saw a guy asleep on the grass near to the mansion. That is not unusual at all but he just caught my attention for some reason.

We stopped to speak to him and, as he rolled over, we saw his face; would you believe it, it's only our prisoner from the jail! Lucky, of course, but as the famous quote – variously attributed to golfers Arnold Palmer, Gary Player and Jerry Barber – has it: 'It's a funny thing: the more I practise, the luckier I get!'

I think it's also fair to say that I can be like a dog with a bone and if someone was wanted or sought for an offence then I would go after them with drive and determination. That could mean coming in a little bit early or going home a little bit late, or spending hours checking addresses.

Most people would only ever go in their loft to put away boxes of junk or get down the Christmas tree. I've spent a fair proportion of my life in other people's lofts looking for wanted people who have a habit of lying under the loft insulation or hiding behind hot-water tanks. I recall one lad who had jumped out of bed and then secreted himself under the loft insulation. Fair to say that he was a little bit scratchy on his way to custody.

Unlike most people, 4 a.m. could be my favourite time of

day. We'd get the team together and we'd set off in convoy to whatever part of town our suspect lived in.

Don't get me wrong, these were never petty criminals, these were the ones who were prolific and did the most harm. They were often the hardest to get hold of. Frequently we'd have a few addresses to check and, resources allowing, we'd surround them all to make sure we didn't miss the target.

I remember one in particular where we had three addresses and, as we knocked at the first one, he came flying out of the back door of the second! The message came over the police radio, 'Sarge, we've got him at our address. He's in cuffs.'

Clearly someone had tipped him off but, unfortunately for him, while he'd been sleeping we'd been hatching a cunning plan and we had it covered.

I was never too keen on doing the rear containment of a property; the fences were not an issue but there was always a chance that you'd stumble into a garden in which you were not the only occupant. It was not uncommon for criminals to use dogs when they were trying to buy themselves some time, or ward off the cops. And I wasn't a massive fan of our four-legged friends.

One particular incident involved a robbery of a cash van. The security guard had pulled up at a local pub on the outskirts of the town and, just as she was getting the case of money out of the van, she was robbed by two men on a motorbike. One of them ran over to her and shouted 'Give me the fucking money!' He grabbed the bag before jumping on the back of the motorbike and they were gone.

As soon as the incident was reported we raced to the scene, flooding the area with police cars, but the bike could have been anywhere by then.

I got hold of our Intelligence Unit and we had a think about who in this part of Ipswich would be good for a job like that. I could only think of a handful and it just so happened that one of them had a girlfriend who was living not too far away.

I drove to the area, parking up just short of the house itself. I had a discreet walk past and located a motorbike, which was covered by a tarpaulin at the side of the house. I checked the bike; it matched the description and the brakes and exhaust were still hot.

I got some extra officers there and we surrounded the house. Now, no weapon had been used in the robbery but these types of offences are high stakes and the offenders are generally dangerous people.

I approached the front door and after a few moments one of the occupants came and answered. He was holding the collar of a massive American bull mastiff. The dog was huge and looked very aggressive. 'Can you put the dog in another room? We need to come in and speak to you.'

'Nah, you can talk to me here. You ain't coming in.' The guy thought that as long as he had that dog with him, we would be stuck outside.

As more officers arrived, I think he realised that we would definitely be coming in and, fortunately, after another minute or two, he put the dog in the kitchen and in we went. He and his mate both got nicked for robbery.

When we searched the house, we found the empty money bag on the hob, smouldering away in an ashtray. They had been trying to burn it to get rid of the evidence but, unfortunately for them, the only part of the bag that survived was the unique barcode!

Once they had been taken to custody the search gained momentum and the jacket and crash helmets were found in the loft. The cash had been hidden all around the house; there was even some in a picture frame hanging on the wall.

As I said, these offences are often committed by the most dangerous offenders and that was reinforced when we searched the loft and found a handgun, complete with ammunition. We'll never know if they had that with them at the time of the robbery but criminals only have guns and ammunition to threaten, hurt or kill people. I guess some people may say it was a lucky result, but I'd rather say that it was good old-fashioned policing; knowing your beat and knowing your crims.

Over the years, I became the go-to man when high-profile arrests needed to be made. I think people trusted me to give it my full attention and, if we did find them, there'd be no mishaps.

I recall one such instance involving a series of really nasty street robberies. In the latest incident the offender had robbed a lone woman walking with her very young child in a pram in broad daylight. The robber tried to grab the handbag from the lady and when she put up a fight, he repeatedly punched her in the face until finally she let go. An abhorrent crime and one that needed to be solved, not only for the victim but also for future victims.

CID got to work and received some information about a possible suspect, a lad who had just come out from prison and had previous for street robberies. I was asked to take a look at it as we were on nights and we had received some information about the area of town in which he may have been staying. The information was weak as it didn't give an actual address and that particular part of the town is densely populated with hundreds of houses and flats. A needle in a haystack.

It got to around 1 a.m. and I suggested to a colleague that we should go down to that area and have a walk round to see what we could find. I remember that we pulled up behind some garages and both got out. Our police uniform is pretty discreet, all black with just a few bits of reflective panelling on the body armour. We decided to put on some plain jackets so we could be even more discreet as we had a stroll through the estate under the cover of darkness. It can be quite an eerie feeling when you're walking through empty streets in the early hours. We'd periodically stop and stand in the street, looking around at the blocks of flats and houses.

Where do you start? As we walked through the area there was a house that had a light on downstairs, which made it stand out as it was the only house with any lights on. As we stood across the road from it a figure appeared in the front room, which was bereft of curtains, and all of a sudden the light went out. That was a little odd and I started to think, 'I just wonder.'

I called up for some additional officers to come to the location and we began to surround the house, desperately hoping that we were in the right place. We did some computer checks on the address and although our suspect was not known to frequent it, the occupant was a fairly shady character so it was worth some attention.

After around ten minutes everyone was in position and we moved in, approaching the front door and knocking. Nobody answered. We knocked again. Still nobody answered. I knew that someone was in as the light had been turned off by the figure we had seen in the front room. I knocked again and shouted through the letterbox, 'Open the door, we know you're inside.' After a few moments there was some movement in the hallway and then the door was opened by a man we knew was the occupant of the house. 'All right, fella, who else is in the flat?'

'Just a mate,' he replied.

'What's his name?' The first name he gave was the same as the lad we were looking for. 'Can you ask him to come and speak to me at the front door?' That fell on deaf ears and he remained motionless at the front door. I think he realised that he was getting involved in something that really didn't involve him at all.

Within a few moments we were inside and the robbery suspect was found hiding behind some boxes in a cupboard. Result. Some would say that, again, this was just good luck. Some would say you make your own luck. I'd say it's a bit of both. The main thing was that a violent, dangerous offender was off the streets and on his way back to jail.

I remember the day after the arrest, a detective inspector sent me an email to thank us for our work and say well done. He also asked me to buy him a lottery ticket – clearly, he thought I was just lucky!

It's also true that I am a really bad loser, probably the worst. In sport, I don't mind if we've played well and lost but if we've played badly then that is not acceptable at all. Policing often feels like that but, unlike sport, when we lose people can get hurt or become the victim of crime.

I remember in 2013 we were trying to hunt down a pair of house burglars who were prolific. I had been involved in arresting them several years earlier for a series of high-value house breaks and, despite serving a number of years in jail, they came out and carried on where they had left off. These were despicable individuals who showed absolutely no regard for their victims, breaking into their homes and stealing their belongings, and they were top of the list of targets for everyone in Ipswich.

One of the suspects was seen in the town centre by an officer and he predictably made off on foot. We got officers there as quickly as we could but he was gone and we lost him. That affected me for days. The thought that we had been so close and yet we'd just missed out. I spent many hours analysing the sighting, reflecting on what we could have done differently and whether we'd blown an opportunity. In reality, he'd got lucky and we hadn't. I think it's important that the public know how much it hurts cops when offenders get away – if it didn't, then I'd question whether the person is doing the right job. I remember a superintendent once telling me, 'Don't beat yourself up, Ali, their day will come.' He was, of course, right but what damage could they do in the meantime?

The same suspect who had got away remained at large for another few days and then we got that bit of luck we'd been missing. I remember it well, as it was my birthday and someone on the shift asked me what I'd like to get as a present. Without hesitation I said that I wanted both of them nicked, that's what I really wanted for my birthday. It had played on my mind since the incident a few days before and it had become the number one priority for me and the team.

A short time later a motorbike made off when the riders saw one of our Armed Response Vehicles, and the suspects on the bike then made a run for it, darting across a road and down an embankment. From the descriptions given, we were fairly confident that it was the two we were looking for. They had been lost near some flats but they were now within an area where there was nowhere to hide and no crowds of people to melt into. It was also not their part of town so we perhaps had a slight advantage.

I arrived on the scene within a few minutes and we ascertained that they were probably somewhere within a block of six flats. I assembled a small army of officers, including a dog unit and a helicopter as I was determined there would be no mishaps this time. This was a golden opportunity to take two dangerous, callous offenders off the streets so it deserved a gold-star service.

Once the officers were in place surrounding the building, we approached the block and predictably the back window of a first-floor flat flew open and a figure appeared, leaning out anxiously. A rather ferocious and hungry looking 'land shark' greeted him, barking aggressively, straining on the lead and no doubt willing him to make a run for it.

Police dogs are incredibly impressive, even more so when you see them up close. The stereotypical German shepherd is feared among the criminal fraternity and rightly so; they seem to have a particular taste for those who decide to run or fight. The window closed as quickly as it had been opened and we now knew the flat we were looking for. I went to the front door, not because it was personal, because it never is, but because it was important.

After a very short time the door opened and both men were arrested without fuss – the game was up. The feeling of satisfaction was immense and in many ways all the more satisfying because of the seriousness of the offences and also the challenges we'd faced in arresting them.

It felt a whole lot better than the near miss a few days before and it was something that the team felt the buzz from for days – this is what all of us joined the police to do.

It's also sometimes the case that you have to wait for your moment. We had a local criminal who had a propensity for stealing cars and he became infamous with both the local police and the local community. It seemed that the deterrent of the courts and going to jail was not enough to stop his insatiable appetite for committing vehicle crime.

It was around the time that the term 'joyriding' was frequently used and it was a major issue. It's a stupid name for it as there is no joy involved and, as we've seen over the years, the trail of death and destruction it can leave behind is almost unimaginable. I don't think the people involved ever fully appreciated the risks they were taking; stealing a car often resulted in a pretty measly sentence, but if you kill someone in the process you'd be going to jail for a very, very long time; not to mention having to live with the guilt for the rest of your life.

This particular offender had recently been through police custody and had been to court for a number of offences. The court had surprisingly released him on bail with conditions to abide by a curfew.

Predictably he took no notice and he'd regularly be seen at other addresses or would not be present at his home when he should have been there. Police can arrest someone for breaching their bail conditions, but almost inexplicably officers aren't allowed to force entry to a home to make the arrest. This lad knew that and on many occasions he'd be seen in other addresses and he'd goad the officers, almost taunting them, knowing that he was untouchable. Or so he thought. We got a call about a stolen car and unsurprisingly it was found on fire near to an address this lad was known to frequent.

Officers arrived along with the fire service and, as you can imagine, a crowd gathered and there was much activity on the estate. It was a summer's evening and the streets seemed to be filled with youngsters running and cycling around, enjoying the show of blue lights.

After a few minutes our man appeared at an upstairs window, once again goading the officers outside. He was revelling in it, giving the officers 'the bird' and engaging with them in fairly basic conversation.

His mates were also loving it; he was their hero and they were watching in admiration. Little did he know that his luck was about to change in spectacular fashion. He'd just been identified as the suspect for stealing that car and, unlike breach of bail, theft comes with the full array of powers to enter an address.

When I heard the news it was with a sense of relief that we'd now be able to take this danger off the streets for one night at least and maybe make a statement in the process.

I remember frantically calling up resources from all over the town; this arrest was probably not going to go down well, particularly with all his loyal supporters in tow, and he often proved elusive. The resources were amassing nearby and it was a case of trying to keep things low key at the scene. As Del Boy would say, 'Play it cool, Trigger, play it cool, my son,' but this time we'd not be falling through the open bar!

I was pretty sure that if we began moving resources nearer to the address then they'd sense that their invincibility was not quite so assured, and I imagined that he'd take his chance to do a runner.

Once I was happy that we had enough people ready to go, we decided to move in en masse. All of a sudden the streets that had been filled with youngsters and onlookers were filled with cars, cops and police dogs. The atmosphere changed very quickly and there was now no noise from the address and no gesturing at the officers; they were battening down the hatches.

In truth, we didn't knock on the door for long; they weren't going to open up so, on command, forward stepped a colleague who promptly kicked the wooden front door off its hinges and in we went. I always found that when we entered addresses like these there was a moment when everyone would weigh each other up; this was no exception but I think they realised that perhaps this was one that they wouldn't bother fighting so, other than the inevitable earache, there was no real hostility. Not surprisingly the guy we were looking for was nowhere to be seen.

We began searching the address when the call came that he was coming out the back. I had learnt very quickly that in this job people are incredibly good at jumping fences! I'd even become pretty efficient over the hurdles myself.

I got downstairs in time to see him hiding in the corner of the garden and as soon as he saw me, he went garden hopping, disappearing over the fence in a flash. The bad news for him was that he met one of our finest officers, who also happened to be an equally fine rugby player, in the next-door garden, and he was promptly tackled through a fence panel and on to the ground.

We'd got our man. He wasn't happy, acting like we'd cheated. We hadn't cheated, we'd played by the rules, however odd they sometimes are, and we'd done what I imagine 99 per cent of the people on that estate wanted us to do; lock up someone who one day could possibly have killed them or one of their family.

This incident was one that lived long in the memory, not because it was complicated or that out of the ordinary but because it would serve as a reminder that we had to keep persevering and, as that superintendent said to me, 'Their day will come.'

Another issue that came out of being so well known, infamous even, was the misinformation and rumours that created among the criminal fraternity.

I recall arresting a young lad for a drunken public order offence. He was a lively chap and en route to custody he barely stopped for breath. I got chatting to him and asked him if he had been arrested before. He had, by Sergeant Livingstone no less; or so he thought. I began to wrack my brain as I couldn't place him at all. 'So what happened when you got nicked by Sergeant Livingstone?'

He began to regale a tale of woe, not dissimilar to the situation he found himself in on this particular night, and then gave his reason for why he had been arrested by Sergeant Livingstone. 'He just doesn't fucking like me. Everyone hates him. I just wish he'd die.'

I was now absolutely sure that we had never met.

On arrival at custody he continued to shout about his previous arrest and that he did not want to see or speak to Sergeant Livingstone ever again or he would knock him out! As we entered the charge room and stood in front of the custody sergeant, I felt the time was right to enlighten this young chap.

As I took the handcuffs off and put them away, I said to him, 'I don't know who you are and I am pretty sure that we've never met, but *I* am Sergeant Livingstone.'

For the first time he was speechless. I then turned and walked away, leaving him with the custody staff. It brought it home to me that I was now someone that people loved to hate, even people who had never met me.

It reminded me of a story that a very well-known criminal told me. He was convinced that any time that a crime was committed on his estate and a vague description was given everyone put his name up for the job. He had a good reason to be perturbed as this often happened when he was in prison or could prove he wasn't in Ipswich at all. I now knew how he felt.

Working in a town the size of Ipswich, there were an awful lot of repeat customers that I arrested. Some of them twenty, thirty, maybe even forty times. With the vast majority I did not have any issues, hopefully because I was fair and decent with people irrespective of what they had allegedly done. As the saying goes, 'Don't hate the player, hate the game', and that was certainly the case for most of them.

Some, however, were not quite so understanding. They took issue with the work that I did and the fact that if they did commit offences, particularly the most serious ones, I would pursue them relentlessly.

That came at a cost and to many people it will have been a hidden cost. Over the years I have suffered some of the most outrageous threats – threats to shoot me and my family, threats to set fire to my house, threats that people will follow me home and threats to stab me off duty.

All front-line cops will get threatened at work, normally when people are angry or drunk or high on drugs. It's like water off a duck's back and I'd often tell them to join the queue of criminals, which for me went right round the block. The more concerning threats were made in the cold light of day, when people were not so pumped up and were thinking more clearly.

I recall one phone call from an offender. 'All right, Livingstone; how are you?'

'I'm good, thanks, what can I do for you?'

He went on to proudly tell me that he knew an awful lot about me.

'I know where you live, I know where your family live, I know that you drive a black Subaru Impreza, I even know where you play squash.'

He offered me a deal; 'I'm in court next week for driving while disqualified. If you get it kicked out then I'll tell you who told me that stuff about you.'

I remember being totally shocked, not only that he thought he knew all of this about me, but also that he thought he'd be able to persuade me to do something corrupt and, frankly, criminal.

The information was all correct but I was never going to tell him that. I told him that it was all wrong and whoever had told him was way off the mark. He then dropped an absolute bombshell.

'That's bullshit, Livingstone, it's all true and I know that because it's a copper who told me.' The lad told me he'd reveal who that was if I got his case dropped.

I told him in no uncertain terms, 'We don't do deals so go fuck yourself!' I slammed the phone down. I was so, so angry. How dare he? And who on earth would betray my trust to such an extent?

The information that he knew was detailed and it was pretty up to date so it was someone who knew me well. As you can imagine, we spent a lot of time and effort trying to find out the source of the information but to no avail. I'm glad for their sakes that no harm came to me or my family; otherwise they may have had a few difficult questions to answer.

For me, that was an extreme example of just how much moral courage is needed to do this job; it was never negotiable and a deal was never on the table, despite what he hoped. He was so smug and thought that by dragging my family's safety into it, and making me believe that another police officer had given him this information, he'd be able to exert some control. I'd just have to factor in the additional risks for a while and make sure that I was on my guard on and off duty.

When I say these threats happened over several years, I really do mean it; it was constant at times and most definitely affected the way I lived my life. I remember one night getting a call at home from a senior detective. 'Is that Sergeant Livingstone?'

'Yeah, speaking.'

He told me that a well-known criminal, who had a particularly deep-seated hatred towards me, had acquired a firearm. 'We felt that you ought to know.'

Just take a moment to think about that: I was called at home at 1 a.m., while sound asleep, to tell me that a criminal I knew well had got a gun and, what's more, an experienced senior officer felt I needed to be aware.

It certainly got my attention and for a long, long time it weighed heavily on my mind. Fortunately, nothing ever came of it, and perhaps they were just being cautious, but it illustrates just how dangerous my life had become.

A lot of officers can live and work in the same town; I couldn't. A lot of officers can go out and socialise in town-centre pubs and bars; I couldn't. A lot of officers can go shopping with friends and family; I couldn't. A lot of officers can go where they please and not give it a second thought; I couldn't. I didn't resent that but it was a reality and something that came with the public service that I did, and I won't be the only officer who has either suffered this themselves or knows someone who has.

For many years I'd feel safer on duty than off duty. When I was at work I had all my personal safety kit, all my colleagues, and I felt strangely calm about my safety. Being off duty was the complete opposite and I'd always be alert and on the look-out for any potential problems.

The most difficult part was that the threats impacted on my family and that was a constant worry as they had not joined the police and yet they were being dragged into my work.

I guess that, because of the number of people I dealt with and my perceived notoriety within the criminal fraternity, it was always going to be more persistent for me. It also perhaps busts the myth that I was just arresting petty criminals for minor offences; most definitely not. These were hardened offenders who were being locked up for serious criminality and as such they were not to be taken lightly.

I found that the people I arrested regularly and who were prolific all had different motivations to commit crime.

Some, a fair number in fact, were dependent on drugs and their offending was as a direct consequence. It led them to commit some of the most despicable crimes, but I always felt a tinge of sadness and regret as very few of them were 'bad' people. They had got into a world of hurt and just couldn't break the cycle. I felt a lot of compassion for them and I'd always try and look out for them and make sure they were treated with respect; their life was hard enough and nothing would have pleased me more than seeing them start again and get free from drugs or alcohol.

Others were just driven by pure greed or thrill seeking. They didn't have addiction as an excuse, they just wanted what they were not prepared to work for. I thought back to my colleague at Ipswich Hospital who had three jobs to make ends meet; she couldn't have been further from some of the people I encountered.

What I would say about my arrests was that it was something that would never have been possible without the amazing colleagues I worked with. I'd often be the annoying colleague who on the way back to the nick at the end of a long, tiring shift would see a person who was wanted and invariably that would mean that some of us would be late off.

I think, though, that all cops want to lock up the people who blight their community and I think that the police must never lose sight of that.

16

Complacency is the enemy of safety

I AM NOT A football fan as such, in fact I've not paid to watch a game live for about twenty years, but I do follow it and if it's on the TV I'm quite happy to sit in the comfort of my own home and spectate. I have, however, spent a huge amount of time dealing with football policing.

Football policing is unique and certainly unlike any other form of event that I've been involved in. The vast majority of the people who attend are decent, law-abiding fans who want to enjoy the match. There are, however, at almost every club, a very small minority who are not decent and on match days may well not be law abiding. In the police they are known as 'risk supporters' and that is appropriate because they do present a risk of anti-social behaviour or violence.

I think that for some the stereotypical risk supporter has been glamorised by movies and documentaries that have exposed their activity and behaviour. It's incredibly frustrating because I've seen younger and younger risk supporters coming to the forefront and, as any cop will tell you, every briefing on football risk groups will talk about a 'youth group'. What a sad state of affairs.

Football policing has been a real focus over many years as the police have strived to improve safety at events. It goes without saying that after any major tragedy lessons must be learnt and, after the Bradford fire and the Hillsborough disaster, it was absolutely right that we did all we could to ensure that never happened again. To that end, as a command trainer I would often run a policing events course, which became a requirement for any match commander to oversee a football fixture.

We'd always open the course with the reasons we were there and we would then put on a video of the Bradford fire. It was one of the worst stadium disasters in Europe. Saturday 11 May, 1985, was a day of celebration for Bradford City as they were crowned champions of the third division.

As the match got underway disaster struck as a fire started in the main stand. Fifty-six people died and 265 were injured.

I've seen the footage countless times and it is still almost unbearable to watch. I would ask the commanders to keep an eye on the clock at the bottom of the screen and as the fire took hold and people ran from the burning stands, the time seemed to almost slow down or even stop. Within five minutes the destruction and death were evident for all to see.

At one point an elderly man came running from the stand, his coat and hair fully alight. Police officers and spectators rush to his aid, frantically trying to beat the flames out with their coats. It is the most harrowing and traumatic footage.

I would then stop the video and the room would be silent; the commanders realising the magnitude of their responsibilities to work alongside the football clubs to make sure that spectators all got home safely.

It's a harsh way to start a course, but we felt it was absolutely right to set the scene and leave people in no doubt: to fail was not an option as lives depended on it. I would also remind them of what Lord Justice Taylor said in his report on Hillsborough: 'complacency is the enemy of safety'. Therefore to be complacent was not an option either.

We then covered the Hillsborough disaster of 1989. It's the most spoken about of all the major fatal sporting events in this country, and the subject has remained intense with the subsequent criminal proceedings and trials of some of the police officers involved.

I sometimes reflect on how, through it all, the fact remains that ninety-six Liverpool supporters went to watch their team play and they never came home. That must never happen again. Some people think it won't happen again; the stadiums are better, the regulations are far more stringent and the police training is far more detailed. I'd often remind people, though, that in Duisburg in Germany in 2010, twenty-one people went to the Love Parade music festival and died as the result of a crush. This was a developed country with similar governance and yet a disaster had unfolded in front of the organisers' very eyes.

Examples such as that show how complex football policing can be, and are a stark reminder that it's not to be taken lightly. The safety of the crowd at large is also far more important than a small amount of disorder. It is about making sure people are safe but also, where possible, that the police can mitigate against the actions of any criminal element who are intent on disorder.

It would be so much easier if the police could just concentrate on the safety aspect and leave people to behave responsibly. Unfortunately, that seems unlikely and football-related disorder will continue and, worryingly, the statistics show it's getting worse.

So who gets involved? Well, it's probably not who you think. At the risk of some generalisations here, they are often in employment (it takes a lot of money to go to football and drink the amount they do) and for the majority of their lives they are law abiding or at least not career criminals.

The hooligan groups themselves will be made up of the minority who really do want to have a punch up and the majority who want to wear designer clothes and confront people but, if it all gets a bit lively, then they will be taking more than a few steps back and looking for the nearest police officer to hide behind.

I remember one incident in particular after an Ipswich match against Leeds United. It was October 2010 and Ipswich got a late winner. The officer I was working with from Leeds turned to me and said, 'Now you're in trouble.' And he was right.

As the match finished the fans spilled out on to the car park opposite where the Leeds United supporter coaches were all parked. Emotions were running high and this was not helped by a few bottles being thrown at the coaches, which were now filling with Leeds fans.

A confrontation soon followed and the police moved in to form a line to prevent the group moving off.

Leeds United fans are well known for being able to handle themselves. The Ipswich risk group then appeared, quietly walking through the crowds, passing their adversaries with heads down and hoods up.

Once safely behind police lines of riot cops and snarling dogs, they began to taunt and threaten the opposition. For me, that summed it up. Maybe if the police weren't there they wouldn't confront each other at all. I guess that's a discussion for another time.

The incident was also memorable because of a conversation

I had with one of the Leeds supporters. He came over to speak to me: 'Excuse me, boss, that was bang out of order, there was no need for that.'

As he was talking I noticed a trickle of blood running down his forehead. 'What was out of order?' I asked.

'All of that, there was no need for all those officers to get their batons out.' As he carried on the trickle of blood was getting more and more obvious. I asked him what had happened to his head.

'Oh that? I was stood at the front and one of my mates pushed me in the back. When I fell forward one of the police dogs bit me.' He leant over so I could see the top of his bald head; there were four puncture marks, all of which were now bleeding.

It made me smile afterwards; he'd been bitten by a police dog on the top of his head but that was fair enough, yet he was not happy that some officers had got their batons out to try and stop a load of blokes having a scrap.

My training and experience of public order also gave me a great insight into some aspects of psychology. I was fascinated by the work of Professor Clifford Stott in relation to crowd behaviour, and particularly how the police could positively influence them.

In years gone past crowds were treated as exactly that; great numbers of people who were all considered as one entity and herded around accordingly. That is just not real: within that crowd there will be many groups and, importantly, thousands of individuals.

In my experience, especially with football and protests, crowds can often be split into three groups. Generally, speaking, there will be a group within the crowd who would never, ever get involved in criminality; no matter what happens they will remain law abiding throughout. There may then be a group within the crowd who are law breakers and they have the intent and capability to do that – they are the ones I've spent the majority of my working life chasing around! And, finally, there is a group in the middle who may either get carried away in the moment and act up or, if they were policed effectively, they'd stay nice and calm. We clearly wanted it to be the latter. There were a number of factors that could influence this and one of the biggest ones was police action.

I remember one incident after a football match where we had spent an hour or more trying to persuade a group of fairly colourful characters to get on a train at Ipswich station and go back to their home town. They finally got on, but the atmosphere was tense and it felt as though it could go off at any moment. The platform was lined with riot cops and police dogs viciously snapping and snarling at anyone who looked in their direction.

As the train was getting ready to depart an officer leapt on board and tried to drag someone out of the carriage and back on to the platform as they'd just damaged a piece of plastic trim. It went ballistic! It was like the blue touch paper had been lit and the group were now trying to fight their way off the train to confront the police.

Barely anyone in that carriage would know why that young lad was being manhandled off the train, but that didn't matter – in their eyes it wasn't justified and that was enough.

Had the officer done anything wrong? Probably not, but perhaps it could have been dealt with slightly differently. Looking at it in the cold light of day, that lad had damaged a piece of plastic trim, which would only cost a couple of quid to repair, but because he'd been nicked the whole situation kicked off.

This is why policing is so tricky; sometimes your actions can be the thing that sets a whole series of events in motion. So what were the alternatives? Turn a blind eye? Wait until he got to the other end and nick him as he got off the train? I think it's fair to say that I'd have preferred that as opposed to the small riot that started.

Within the football context this model works quite well and fortunately the majority of the crowd are law abiding and will not commit offences. There will always be a group in the middle who may go either way and there may, unfortunately, be some law breakers.

I always felt that on any given day the hooligan groups would not be there to commit offences, they just enjoyed the spectacle of it all. There will be people far more intelligent than me who feel this is too simplistic and doesn't fit all situations but as a starting point it has real validity and, as a practitioner, I have seen it in action over many, many years.

The other thing that it showed me is that there are varying degrees of risk supporter. I guess that makes sense as risk does go up and down and no two groups will be the same.

There are clubs that are feared up and down the country and there are some risk groups who won't bother travelling if they don't think the opposition are up to much.

I recall one season Glasgow Rangers came to Ipswich for a pre-season friendly. They had a fearsome reputation and rightly so; battle-hardened over many years of disorder with Celtic and Aberdeen.

The match was a bit of a non-event but the risk groups both turned out in good numbers. But there was never a chance of Ipswich fans wanting to take on Rangers, not even on home soil.

I was the night-turn sergeant that evening and as midnight approached I was informed that the two public order vans that had been on for the football were going to stand down and go off duty. That seemed OK as there wasn't much going on and, apart from a few of the Ipswich risk group in a local nightclub, all appeared well.

In hindsight it was the wrong decision. I was sitting in my car outside the nightclub along with a few colleagues and, all of a sudden, we heard chanting coming from further up the road.

Within a few moments we could see it was a large group of Glasgow Rangers supporters, marching straight up the middle of the road. They weren't strolling along; they were on a mission.

I had never seen such a reaction from our own risk group, the ones who had come out of the nightclub were trying to get back in and the ones who couldn't were trying to find a police officer to protect them. It was like a scene from *Scooby-Doo* when the dog jumps into Shaggy's arms.

The Rangers group went through the street like a dose of salts, assaulting members of the public as they went; then, as quickly as they'd appeared, they disappeared into the night. It was a valuable lesson, as when people talked about risk supporters, the assumption is that they generally drink a lot and will try and confront their opposition, but it's important to remember: what is their capability and what is their true intent?

I've been involved in many of the derby matches between Ipswich and Norwich. For a derby, the clubs are sometimes quite a long way apart, but the hatred and animosity are toxic.

Cops would often get their first taste of policing football at one of these derbies, as it generally seemed the entire force had their rest day cancelled and were working it.

I really enjoyed it but I can imagine that some officers could think of nothing worse than a long, hard day of trying to keep warring factions apart. And I guess from a commander's point of view they are particularly challenging as the risk groups can double in size and double again as people who would never normally turn up at football and get involved in disorder decide to give it a go on derby day.

The planning for these operations would take many weeks and the logistics involved are considerable as the resources were often brought in from all over the region.

I recall one derby in particular, which was on a Bank Holiday weekend with an evening kick-off. The police or the club can make a request for a match to be played at an alternative time if they feel it will improve safety. Unfortunately, this match took place as planned and when I arrived at one bar and found that it was full at 11 a.m., I anticipated it was going to be tough.

I was a football spotter on the day. Our task was to find the risk groups and keep tabs on them.

The relationship between spotters and risk is generally OK, as there is an understanding that at some point they will need our help. Particularly when groups travel to away fixtures, they would often want some support to make sure they all got home safely!

On a derby day such as this, being a spotter is hard work as you walk miles and miles and while the supporters are in the pubs drinking, you're standing outside on your feet all day. Predictably the match was a nightmare and it resulted in significant disorder, a throwback to the bad old days, but the objective was achieved and everyone got home in one piece.

Another incident that springs to mind as a football spotter was when Ipswich travelled to Millwall. There will not be many people who follow football who do not know about the Millwall risk group – the infamous Bushwhackers.

The Ipswich risk group turned out in decent numbers, as was often the case for matches in the capital; it's a short trip on the train and a chance to see the bright lights of the city.

It's fair to say that there was a lot of grandstanding and posturing by the Ipswich group, but they were always keen to know that their friendly Suffolk officers were there to keep them safe.

I've followed risk groups around for many years and I've never been attacked or set upon; perhaps it is the fact that they need us and we certainly don't need them. That seems a ridiculous thing to say, as they'd often tell us to leave them alone, but it's genuinely how I felt – there was no way that they would come off on top if they bumped into a couple of hundred Millwall yobs so they wanted to keep us in sight at all time. Curious really, as we were actually there to keep an eye on them.

I also travelled to Düsseldorf for a pre-season fixture. It was a tough job but someone had to do it! It was also an amazing chance to see how another country deals with football.

In Germany drunk supporters are allowed into the ground, so some of our fans took advantage of it; the mix of sun and alcohol resulted in the majority of them being asleep at the back of the stand by the time kick-off came around.

It was also interesting to see the spotting operation. It's a bit less intrusive and very passive in its nature. The risk group from Düsseldorf were formidable; they looked big, strong and were sporting more than a few scars. They looked battle ready.

Some of the Düsseldorf risk group approached our German colleagues and made them aware they had heard that Ipswich had brought fifty people to fight.

Our German colleagues queried that with us and we pointed to the handful of drunks asleep in the stands. They were not here to fight; they were here to drink and watch some football.

After that interaction with the police, the Düsseldorf group began being deployed by their leader: they were splitting up all over the place to make sure that they would encounter their perceived adversaries. It was like a military operation.

My colleague and I were there to observe and help the German police but their lack of action or attentiveness caused us some real concern, though we appreciated it was their operation, not ours.

Had this been in the UK, the obvious preparations being made by the risk group would have resulted in hurried activity from the police – moving police officers into position and getting evidence gatherers with their video cameras in the right place to make sure that if it did kick off it would all be captured in high definition.

Evidence gatherers were often seen at football fixtures, working in pairs with a video camera to capture any indiscretions. On the whole, they had a really calming, sobering effect and it certainly made a few people think before they acted.

As the game came to an end the Ipswich supporters began leaving the stadium to walk to a party that had been planned at a nearby venue. The atmosphere was really good and the fans were in fine spirits but there was clearly some nervousness as they had seen the group from Düsseldorf.

As we left the ground, we made our way along the route in the car and could see that the Düsseldorf risk group had taken over a pub and were waiting outside, lining the pavement. I was now really worried and I could see that not only our risk group but all the other supporters would have to run the gauntlet.

We explained our concerns to our counterparts but it didn't really prompt the response we'd have got in the UK where there would have been an overt display of police resources to ensure there was no disorder.

My colleague and I decided we'd have to go over, so we tentatively got out of our vehicle conscious that we were dressed like the vast majority of other supporters and we were in a foreign land with no kit and no real support.

We walked over just as our risk group came stumbling up the road, but even through their drunken haziness I think the sight of the Düsseldorf group lining their route sobered them up pretty quick. Fortunately, on this occasion there was no disorder and after some words were exchanged, I think they agreed that this was not the day for fighting.

It was a trip that certainly made me consider our approach to policing football and it showed that we're not that far off the mark. I guess that's why at most major tournaments in Europe the UK police send representatives to help their overseas colleagues manage the risks. And, unlike many others, British police officers are quite happy to start with some talking rather than moving quickly to water cannon and tear gas!

I can't overemphasise, though, that the vast majority of football fans are good people. In Suffolk I think that we dealt with visitors to the town very well and ensured that they felt safe and reassured.

I hope that as time goes on the role of police at football will get smaller and smaller, and we can leave it with the football clubs to manage their own events like almost all other organisers.

17

It's my right!

IF THERE IS one thing that cops love, it's the chance to go on an away day. I don't really know why because often they are hard: long days, long hours and long journeys. Despite this, I was with the majority and some of my most memorable experiences happened when we travelled to other parts of the UK to police various events.

When I got wind of the fact that police from the mainland would be involved in policing the G8 Summit in Northern Ireland in 2013 I was most definitely up for that!

This highlights just how little I knew about other places and communities, and I don't think that I am alone on that front.

The political situation in Northern Ireland is, from my perspective, very complex and extremely challenging. Like so many others, I will follow significant developments on the news and am loosely aware of the conflicts and differences but it's not something that affects my daily life, so when I found out we were going over to assist it was time to pay more attention.

As a teenager, I remember meeting a lad who played squash for Ireland and, while stranded in a European airport, he and I sat and talked politics. He spoke with such astounding knowledge and passion about the parties involved. I was totally taken aback by how much he knew about it as we were both only fifteen or sixteen years old, but why wouldn't he know about it? It was a fundamental part of his life.

The G8 Summit was going to be in a beautiful part of Northern Ireland but, as with all political meetings of this nature, the chance of protest was high.

A couple of years earlier London had endured the G20 Summit and the protests that went with that. This was different, though, as the policing landscape in Northern Ireland is, in many respects, unique and it was by no means a foregone conclusion that the protest groups would attend in any great numbers.

We were taking no chances, though, so we all headed off to some bespoke public order training as the tactics and equipment used over there were very different to those we were used to. For a start, the vehicles all had to be bulletproof and the risk of explosive devices was higher than almost anywhere else in Europe. Why did I want to go again?

The training was exceptional. It was my first look at the Police Service of Northern Ireland (PSNI) and I think I can safely say that they are the most professional group of people I encountered during my service. They are clearly battle-hardened and operate in an arena filled with threat and risk, but they take it in their stride and they work as a team.

Perhaps it was the stories they told or the way they carried themselves but I left the training thoroughly motivated and thinking, *If they can manage what they've got to deal with and still have that can-do, positive attitude, why on earth can't we?*

We flew into Belfast and immediately got up to speed with the environment that we would be operating in. We were met in a secure area and, before we knew it, we were in the Land Rovers and on the way to the military base.

The Land Rovers were in many respects the best and worst thing about this operation. They were the best because when you were in them you felt safe and secure, and most definitely a unit. They were the worst because they were small, cramped, smelly and very hot! The PSNI may be highly professional and incredibly welcoming, but they weren't daft so the vehicles we were given were definitely not the pride of the fleet.

On arrival at the military base we were briefed on our deployments and it was pretty clear, pretty quickly, that we were there to assist with the security operation and that it was highly unlikely that there would be much protest at all.

The next week was spent working some long, long hours with not a lot to amuse a bunch of highly motivated and keen public order officers. I remember our point well as we spent the best part of sixteen hours a day there. It was a lovely country track, next to a big old country house overlooking rolling hills and countryside. Idyllic. Our unit was around a mile from the golf resort where the summit was taking place so we saw all the big guns flying in – Barack Obama and Vladimir Putin being the highlights.

So what does a public order unit do for sixteen hours a day when there is nothing to do? Well, a fair proportion of it was spent eating and then the challenges started. I had a great team of officers whom I'd known and worked with for many years in Ipswich. I recall one particular afternoon deciding that we'd have a press-up challenge – it all sounds very macho but it wasn't, it was just something to pass the time. If anyone was watching – and I'm pretty sure people will have been – it must have been the strangest thing to see.

It reminds me of a story that one of my old inspectors told me from his time working in the Met. They were all deployed as part of a public order situation and, much to the frustration of the cops, it went on and on and on. This was in the days before digital hi-tech police radios so it was impossible to know who was transmitting unless they gave their unique callsign or you recognised their voice.

After a number of hours an officer called up on the radio, 'I'm bored.'

The unit commander responded immediately in a slightly irritated tone, 'Please maintain your radio discipline.' In layman's terms this means, *Behave!*

A few more minutes passed and then the same disgruntled officer called up on the radio, 'I'm still bored.'

The unit commander was now starting to lose his temper. 'That last officer, identify yourself immediately.'

After a few seconds the officer called up for a third and final time, 'I said I was bored, not stupid!'

This was met with raucous laughter from the various police vans all around the city. I can only imagine the anger coursing through the unit commander's veins, but hopefully after the event he will have seen the funny side.

And then in Northern Ireland there was the accommodation. Never before and hopefully never again will I have to reside in a 'snooze pod'. It is a tiny room that has two sets of bunk beds, but the beds are only a couple of feet apart so space is nonexistent. That was home for me and my three roommates for a week. It was grim and I'm pretty sure that they are called snooze pods because, with three other blokes grunting, snoring and farting, there was absolutely no chance of getting any proper sleep. And you can't even begin to imagine the smell; generally, cops don't eat particularly well when on tour: add in a few pints of Guinness each evening and it was not pretty.

Following the G8 Summit we all headed home after what had been an interesting experience. Amazingly, only a few months later I got the call that we were going back to Northern Ireland and this time it was to police the 12 July parades. The date is very significant to the Orange Order as it commemorates the Battle of the Boyne of 1690. Some Protestants remember it as a great victory over Catholics and for that reason it can be a highly charged and emotional time, especially when Protestant marchers pass through Catholic areas.

I had no idea about the parades but having looked up some facts and read some reports it became clear that this was going to be a completely different experience – no more sitting around the beautiful countryside, this was going to test our training and resilience to the maximum.

To prepare us for the deployment we were taken to a training centre for some refresher training. It was much needed as the tactics are slightly different to those used on the mainland and it was very obvious that we might actually need to use some of what we had been taught. I recall a briefing by an officer from the PSNI in which he quipped that in Northern Ireland there are five seasons – spring, summer, autumn, winter and riot season, and we had arrived just in time for that!

We were given an idiot's guide to the issues at hand and then we headed off to our military base once more. This had a very different feel to it. The risks were high and if we didn't switch on people might have got hurt; after all, we were police officers from the mainland policing one of the most challenging events you could come across.

On the first day I was asked by the Inspector to accompany him to a briefing in which we would be given our deployments and learn more about the intelligence picture.

As I had come to expect, the briefing was concise, businesslike and straight talking, and it left nothing to the imagination.

I remember listening intently for our callsign to be mentioned. Our location would be 'Crumlin Road and the Ardoyne shops'.

Now, I was still a complete beginner in terms of Northern Ireland and the locations, but even I had heard of Crumlin Road and the Ardoyne shops; in fact, I recalled passing the sign at the entrance to the military base, which advised service personnel to avoid that area. There must have been a mistake as we had been told that we would not be used in any contentious or high-risk areas. No, no mistake; that was where we were going on 12 July.

For those, like me, who don't understand the parades and how they work, on 12 July a large number of parades take place in which the Orange Order march into the centre of Belfast and then at the end of the day they march back out. There is a Parades Commission who can impose restrictions and conditions on the parades and our parade, the one going down Crumlin Road, had some such conditions. It restricted the numbers that could be within the parade and also determined that as it passed the shops themselves there could only be a single drum beat. Controversially there would be no return parade. I felt that I now knew enough to police this and, of course, we would be supported by colleagues from the PSNI.

Our local guides from the PSNI were outstanding and ever so obliging. Everything that they did seemed to revolve around survival – checking under their cars, not frequenting certain locations, not telling people what they did for a living.

It was so alien to the mainland cops and yet the minute we landed it became normal to us as well. I recall one conversation with the PSNI officers who were working with us about what it meant if the crowd started to part in front of us. We said that it would probably mean that a vehicle was coming through, perhaps an ambulance or another police unit. The officer looked across at me and said, 'Aye, you're right, it might be, but it's more likely that it's someone at the back about to start firing at us!'

If they didn't have everyone's attention before that they did now – they had our full and undivided attention! It felt like we were going to war.

On the morning of 12 July we set off early – really early – and drove into Belfast. Some parts looked really quite nice, modern and welcoming, but others looked the complete opposite.

We arrived at the police station and after a quick briefing we headed out to our position for the day. The Bronze Commander was an inspector and he looked and spoke as though he'd policed this part of the world for the last thirty years and he'd been there, seen it and done it. That was of some relief as the Bronze Commander would be with us all day and it was his job to give us our deployments. He would have to skilfully manoeuvre the right resources into the right place at the right time! Sounds easy.

He took us on a walk round to show us the lie of the land and explain the deployments for the day. He reassuringly told us that the morning would be fine: the band would arrive and form up but there would be no disorder or issues; that would all come later in the evening. It was good to know, as it would allow us to gradually get into the deployment and find our feet.

A couple of hours later, as the Bronze Commander had predicted, the band arrived, but we had problems, big problems. Hundreds of people arrived and the atmosphere was toxic.

People began congregating in the road, arguing and shouting about the restrictions that had been imposed. Before I knew it we had the Land Rovers across the road and we were taking missiles – bottles, stones and cans were being thrown at the vehicles.

We were ordered into Code 1, which in layman's terms means riot helmets and shields. People came to the front of the Land Rovers, shouting obscenities at an alarming rate.

I recall an elderly man shouting, 'It's my right', over and over again with such conviction and venom.

I stood at the back of my Land Rover, watching the officers forming up and covering the width of the road, while a young male climbed onto the roof of another Land Rover and began trying to rip the CCTV camera off its boom.

I turned to my right and there was the Bronze Commander, fag in his mouth. He looked directly at me and said, 'Now we're fucked!' I guess that meant we had not expected this quite so early in proceedings.

After a few minutes, though, things started to settle down a little and as I walked round the side of the vehicle to check on the team, I had the bizarre experience of bumping into the actor Ross Kemp, who was there with a film crew. I was more used to seeing him behind the bar of the Queen Vic pub in Albert Square on *EastEnders* and here he was stood in the middle of Belfast during the start of a riot.

I said, 'Good morning,' and he reciprocated before heading off to find someone to speak to or a better vantage point.

After a short time a deal was struck and the band, along with the right number of supporters, set off down Crumlin Road towards the Ardoyne shops, and we were able to relax for a while at least. It had been such a strange few hours and clearly unexpected according to the Bronze Commander.

The rest of the day was relatively quiet for us, which was lucky as the heat was absolutely unbearable. We were in full riot kit including fireproof undergarments, which are exceptionally good at keeping heat out but unfortunately very good at keeping body heat in.

There were cops lying under Land Rovers having water poured all over them just to try and stay hydrated and cool.

Then came the next phase – the return parade. The Parades Commission had of course decided there was to be no return parade and as the day progressed it became clear that this was going to be a major issue for us. We were to remain in our position to prevent supporters of the parade heading down to the Ardoyne shops to bring the parade back. This seemed fairly straightforward and I thought we'd be able to handle that no problem at all.

We set up the vehicles and as I turned and looked down the long, straight road towards the shops I could see two water cannons being positioned in the carriageway. We hadn't seen them up until this point but it seemed that they were being made ready for action.

I listened intently to the police radio to hear when the parade was approaching the key junction and as this was happening the numbers in front of our vehicles continued to grow. It felt like we were going to reach an inevitable tipping point at some stage and it didn't take long.

All of a sudden the radio transmissions from the other end of the Crumlin Road began to increase in number and intensity – they had disorder, serious disorder.

Another Bronze Commander called up on the radio, 'I've got an unconscious officer down, I need further assistance.'

Before the control room operator could respond, a further update, 'I now have two officers down.'

The operator calmly told the commander that they had no additional resources in a position to reach them and they had to deal with what they had.

The commander came back on the radio, 'Officers are now being attacked with swords, we require water cannon and baton gunners.'

I was stood around a half a mile from where this was all happening and my blood ran cold. Never before had I felt such fear that colleagues were about to be killed. They were being attacked with swords, officers were unconscious and there didn't appear to be any way of getting more officers to them.

I turned and now saw the two water cannons revving their engines and heading off towards the other end of Crumlin Road. I desperately hoped that they would be able to help.

The transmissions kept coming and over the next few minutes and hours it was clear that the officers were literally fighting for their lives and fighting for the lives of their colleagues.

Strangely, though, it all seemed very calm and almost business as usual for the PSNI officers. The driver of my Land Rover was someone I had known for many, many years and had worked with in Ipswich. He is a hard man, the sort of guy that you'd take with you to any hint of physical confrontation and someone you could rely on 100 per cent. He had been an officer in the Met Police and he turned to me and said, 'This is worse than the Brixton riots.' That didn't fill me with confidence and reaffirmed my perspective that to get out of Belfast in one piece would be a successful day's work.

We were finally relieved from our responsibilities at around 3 a.m. and we then began to drive out of the city.

We had been on the go for almost twenty-four hours solid and yet there was no hint of flagging, far from it, in fact: we felt like we could keep going for another twenty-four hours. It's amazing what adrenaline can do.

We were still hearing updates from Crumlin Road, as the disorder continued long into the night, and as we headed on to the motorway, black smoke billowed up from fires that had been set all around the city. It had felt like a war zone all day and this made it all the more dramatic. But we had survived and fortunately so too did all the other officers, despite a few injuries and some of the most horrific violence you could see.

We later learnt that the 12 July parades in 2013 were among the worst seen in Belfast since the Good Friday Agreement.

They were also the first time that the PSNI had called on help from UK mainland police forces. Over four hundred officers from the mainland were deployed. During the disorder over twenty rubber bullets were fired and thirty-two officers were injured. Some people may not think that sounds a lot, but to put it in context, during the riots on the mainland in 2011, not a single rubber bullet was fired. In fact, to my knowledge I don't recall an incident when they have ever been used during disorder on the mainland. Not your average day at the office.

A few days later, we returned to the location where the parade had been prevented from passing. It had become a focal point and each evening people would gather there. It now had a completely different feel to it, and the high risk of disorder was gone.

We parked our vehicles up and got out on foot, never straying too far from the sanctuary of the Land Rover. Our guides from the PSNI were ever alert and always on hand with their firearms ready if required.

The road was covered in paint and scorch marks from the disorder on the 12th. While we stood surveying the scene in the early evening sunshine there was suddenly a loud bang. It was as though time stopped and we all froze.

The officer from the PSNI nearest to me bellowed, 'Ballistic cover,' and this sparked us into life and we all ran.

We got to the Land Rover, piled into the tiny space in the back and locked the doors. The bang was a pipe bomb that had been thrown by a youth and had detonated a short distance from our vehicles.

The youth was long gone and fortunately the second device he had thrown did not detonate. Having a pipe bomb thrown at your police vehicle is hopefully a once-in-a-lifetime experience.

My time working with the PSNI was incredible. I returned to Ipswich full of admiration and respect for what they do. They are the most professional, can-do officers I have ever worked with and, in the face of exceptional risks and challenges, they achieve so much.

I arrived back to work and thought, *We really need to take a leaf out of their book to do things more professionally and with a far more positive attitude.*

18

I think there is a child inside

WORKING WITHIN THE emergency services means Christmas has a completely different context. I think that over my service I worked almost every Christmas Day in one form or another. Personally, I like it and you always get to spend some of the day with family and friends.

On Christmas Day 2015 I was working a late shift, so I spent the morning with friends and family and then travelled the 100 miles back to start work at 3 p.m.

Generally late shifts on Christmas Day are not great – by that stage people are realising that they actually don't like each other that much and they are becoming a little tired and irritable. It can end up being a series of domestic arguments and drunken fighting – all very festive!

We would also have some really challenging incidents around Christmas as a lot of people who don't have the support of a family or friends can become very depressed and struggle to cope with life.

I remember one year I was the custody sergeant in Ipswich and the cell block was full of people who were finding life tough, perhaps missing a late mother or father, or not being able to spend Christmas with their children. I recall the overwhelming dark cloud that seemed to envelop the station.

This particular year was no different and the shift started with a steady stream of emergency calls.

Before we really got going, I managed to drop in to see some friends who live in Ipswich and they kindly fed me. It's quite common that on Christmas Day officers will visit family and friends but they know that at any minute they may be called upon to break away and go to an incident. It was a short time after I'd finished eating that an incident came in involving a drunk man threatening a shopkeeper.

The man told the shopkeeper that he was off home to get a gun and then he'd come back and shoot him. The man was someone we knew well and he could be particularly difficult to deal with, and often pretty violent. Although I was sceptical as to whether he actually had a gun, we didn't want him to get the chance to return to the shop so Armed Response Vehicles were summoned to assist.

Before they had arrived we received an update from the officer at the shop – the man was on his way back down the road and was now striding along the pavement with a carrier bag in his hand. He hadn't had the bag earlier so perhaps he had gone and got a gun after all.

I was nearby with a colleague, Ali Maidment. He was the officer who helped save the man's life on the car-park roof a few years earlier. Once again, the moment was now and there was no time to wait as we had an officer in the shop on her own and there was a chance the man had a firearm.

We were within a few seconds of the shop so began to drive towards the location and fortuitously approached the man from behind.

We hatched a plan: we would pull up on the pavement and ask no questions – it was a case of get hands on and get control. A bit of shock and awe. If he turned and pointed a gun at us? Well, we'd cross that bridge when we got there.

Fortunately, the plan worked well and within seconds of us arriving the man was restrained, handcuffed and pinned against the glass window of a neighbouring shop.

A lot of time and effort goes into training officers in all sorts of armlocks and wristlocks, but invariably it all goes out of the window. Fortunately, Ali and I are both big strong guys and as I pulled the man's arms behind his back, my colleague was snapping a handcuff on before the suspect knew what was going on.

A good result and no harm done. Incidentally, the bag he had didn't contain a gun after all: he was full of beer and hot air.

Due to his behaviour I decided to drive up to custody and just make sure that things went to plan and there were no issues. Fortunately, it went well and he was pretty calm about it all, so a short time later I gave Ali a shout on his radio and collected him from custody to take him back to his police car.

I enjoy spending time with Ali, so as we approached the town centre I suggested that we stay out a bit longer and we'd have a float around the town. This decision was about to become very significant.

A short time later the control room called me up to let me know that the fire service were attending a house fire in Ipswich. At the same time the mental health nurse who works with the police called up to say that they too had received a call from a woman saying that she had set fire to her house and was trapped inside.

I turned to Ali. 'We're only round the corner, we're going to that.'

Although we were not being requested by the fire service, we might have been able to help. The police have legal obligations to save life – in fact, there is an expectation that the police take positive action to safeguard people and to be passive would be unlawful. Above all, we have a moral obligation: it's the right thing to do even if it involves taking some personal risks.

We were only around a minute from the address, so as we began hammering through the town we agreed a plan of action.

I said to Ali, 'When we get there, you find the address and I'll get the entry kit.' This comes in the form of a big red metal battering ram that we use to smash down doors and is called an enforcer. It sounds a pretty primitive piece of kit and it is really.

As we drove flat out through the deserted streets, I desperately hoped that by the time we arrived the fire service would already be on scene and we would be there to support them.

When we reached the secluded close it was obvious that we were the first to arrive. Ali leapt from the passenger seat and he was off, running across the grass to locate the house.

I ran to the back of the police car and by the time I had got the enforcer and fire extinguisher out I too had located the house: it was pretty obvious – there was smoke now billowing out of the open upstairs bedroom window.

I ran across the grass and immediately started hitting the door. There is a problem with enforcers – they are great for wooden doors and throwing through windows but the new, modern, secure-by-design UPVC doors are a lot more challenging. Unfortunately, these doors are incredibly effective and often they can prove too much for an enforcer as the door and frame flex and bounce.

We were not in the luxurious position of having a hydraulic ram or something to pick the lock so this was going to come down to brute force and lots of determination. Full of adrenaline, I began hitting the door with all my might. I hit it once and then again and then again. On the third or fourth strike I lost my footing and slipped on the wet paving slab, falling flat on my back. In almost any other circumstance this would have caused much hilarity but this was not any other incident, this was as serious as it gets.

Fortunately, I had dropped the enforcer to the side and Ali immediately picked up where I had left off. Ali is a big guy: he stands over six-foot-four tall and would have been a heavyweight boxer.

I don't think I'd made a great deal of progress with the door and I feared that we would not be able to get in, so I called up on the radio, demanding the Armed Response Vehicle attend with additional entry equipment and telling the control room that the house was on fire.

'We need the ARV now, we can't get in and the house is well alight.' In reality both Ali and I knew that waiting for more equipment was not going to be an option: the bedroom was completely on fire and we fully believed the woman was trapped inside.

'Come on, man, keep going!' I encouraged my colleague.

Ali absolutely annihilated that front door. I can't recall a more impressive entry. Hit after hit after hit on full throttle. I can't remember how many hits it was, but it was probably fewer than ten, and we were in through the mangled remnants of the door and frame.

The hallway was dark, there were no lights on downstairs and it was now full of smoke. I had my torch in one hand and a fire extinguisher in the other. I'm not sure what I hoped to achieve with a small half-empty fire extinguisher but it made me feel better knowing I had it.

I began to check downstairs and came across a living room of dogs, which I promptly sprayed with the extinguisher as they bounded towards me, clearly agitated by the banging on the front door.

Ali went to search the smoke-filled rooms upstairs, with the fire continuing to grow in ferocity. As I finished checking the ground floor, he came stumbling back down. 'She's not down here!' I shouted.

The smoke was oppressive and suffocating, and he was struggling to breathe. 'I can't check all the rooms, the smoke's too thick.'

I decided to give it a go. The woman must be upstairs, as she was not downstairs and, as I've said before, I would always rather try and fail rather than not try at all.

I ran up the stairs and the heat and smoke hit me well before I got to the top. *Fucking hell, it's too much*, I thought.

I sunk to my knees and then on to my front, now lying on my stomach at the top of the stairs. The heat was unbelievable. It was coming from the front bedroom, which was clearly where the fire was.

My biggest concern was what would happen if I went any further. In that split second I contemplated getting lost in the smoke, being overcome and perishing. I nervously hung on to the top of the banister, anchoring myself to something I knew would orientate me back to safety.

While lying on my front, trying to stay under the smoke and heat, I managed to reach across the floor with my right hand and I could feel a lifeless body slumped in the doorway of the bedroom. I had found her!

Before I could do anything, I had to move back towards the top of the stairs – the heat was just too much.

I shouted to Ali, 'I've found her, she's up here.'

This initial elation was short lived and within a split second it became the worst part for me. We had found the casualty; we knew where she was but we might not be able to get her out. How could we leave her now?

I decided to give it another go so I got the extinguisher prepared and took a deep breath. I then went back into the hall, still on my front and blasted the extinguisher towards the bedroom.

I then discarded the extinguisher, grabbed the woman and dragged her to the top of the stairs where I was met by my colleague.

We both instinctively knew what to do. There was no time to do anything other than get her out, now.

We grabbed her clothing and pulled her down the steps. I don't think her feet touched the ground, she was propelled down the stairs and out into the cold night air.

Once we were a few feet outside, we put her down on the wet grass and tried to catch our breath.

Within seconds the upstairs windows blew out and glass showered down around us. Perhaps it would be a good idea to get a bit further back! We grabbed her again and pulled her across the grass.

At this point a neighbour came running over to help us.

As he got to where we were crouching, he shouted, 'I think there is a child inside.'

It stopped Ali and me in our tracks, literally stunned us. I looked at Ali and he looked at me.

Ali said, 'We're going in, we've got to.'

We had just got out but had no choice: we were definitely going back inside.

As this was still computing, I heard the sirens coming up the road. It was the fire service.

I ran towards the road, frantically flagging them down and shouting at the vehicle as it shuddered to a halt. I screamed, 'We've got her out but there is a child inside.'

'Boys, there's a child inside, let's go, let's go,' shouted a fireman to his colleagues. The fire service were amazing. They were kitted up with breathing apparatus and ready as soon as the engine stopped, flying into action. Without hesitation they went inside.

It was at this point that the events began to take their toll – I was struggling for breath, as was Ali, and the woman we had rescued appeared to be unresponsive on the grass.

Fortunately, other people were able to provide first aid to the woman, leaving me to crawl around the wet grass, coughing and retching. It was the strangest feeling: I could breathe but I just couldn't stop coughing uncontrollably.

I stripped off my body armour and threw it on the floor in the vain hope that it would in some way help. It didn't.

After a while, I was joined by a colleague who gave me some water and then the fire service provided me with oxygen. Then we got the news, 'There's nobody else in the house, the kid's not there tonight.'

'Thank God for that!' I exclaimed. It was a sense of sheer relief and jubilation. Any incident involving a child dying is the most traumatic and to think that there had been a young life in the house was almost too much to bear as we would have been so close to finding them.

The fire had now taken hold and the fire service spent some time dousing the flames and preventing it from spreading to nearby properties. It was amazing how quickly they got it under control.

The woman was alive. She had regained consciousness and she was off to hospital with the ambulance crew. In truth, I was feeling so rough that I had no idea what was going on initially – my priority was now most definitely me.

I stood back, looking at the scene for a moment. The windows smashed, the light cream render burnt and scorched, and the front door smashed to smithereens. It seemed completely surreal to think that we had been in there only a few minutes earlier.

Despite not feeling great, I wanted to go and take a look inside. It is fair to say that the damage caused by fire can be almost incomprehensible: the blackened walls, the burnt-out shells of furniture and the unforgettable smell.

I stood at the top of the stairs and saw the fire extinguisher that I had so tightly gripped as I ran towards the fire, now discarded on the burnt carpet. How Ali had checked any rooms is still a mystery and is testament to his determination and will to save the occupant's life.

I came back outside and found Ali, and we got back in the car to leave. 'We're getting too old for this, man,' I said to my friend. We both agreed. Not to mention that sooner or later our luck was bound to run out.

The following day I remember waking up and my throat was excruciatingly sore, so sore that I could barely swallow any fluids let alone eat anything.

I went to A & E, only to see the queue coming out the door, so I called 111 and got to see a doctor at the local surgery.

I was suffering quite badly, as my throat was red raw from the smoke and coughing, and I was in need of medication to try and calm it down. As I very hoarsely explained to the doctor what had happened her eyes widened and she listened intently. I think she felt I was lucky to be in the state that I was and not any worse. She explained that an awful lot of bad things are in smoke, particularly when things inside a house burn; chemicals that could make you very poorly. She'd made her point and I would be taking things easy for a bit.

It was a tough few days of excruciating pain and discomfort, but without trying to sound dramatic about it, I was alive to tell the tale and that could have been so, so different.

As is so often the case, it's after the event that you start to really contemplate what has happened. Earlier in the day I had been with my family watching them open presents and enjoying a Christmas meal and then only a few hours before this incident I was with friends, catching up with them and having a laugh and a joke. Little did I know what was about to happen.

The incident was deliberate, no doubt about that. The woman had even made the call to the fire service herself. She had intentionally set fire to her house in an attempt to kill herself and, in the process, she had almost killed me and my colleague. It would be easy to feel very angry about that and some people, a lot of people, commented very negatively about her and what she had done. The fire could so easily have spread to the adjoining houses and there could have been loss of life. Personally, I feel no animosity at all. I feel great pity for her. For someone to feel so desperate, at such a loss, to set fire to their own house in an attempt to end their life means that they are clearly in a terrible place.

I am also sure that but for our intervention she would have died, but she didn't. We were the right cops in the right place at the right time with the right kit. For all those things to be in place says to me that she deserves a second chance.

She was subsequently convicted at Crown Court of arson with intent or being reckless as to whether life was endangered. It was a pretty straightforward case so Ali and I didn't have to give evidence, although our statements were read out in court. The woman was sent to prison for forty months.

When she was sentenced the judge commended our bravery, which was nice to hear, but I can confidently say it was the most frightening incident I had dealt with in sixteen years of service so I certainly didn't feel brave. I genuinely hope that she gets the help she needs, and she feels ready to take life on and get back to a better place.

19

Please don't do it

It is not uncommon for the police to be involved in a stand-off. In fact, it happens every day to a greater or lesser extent but on occasions these can become protracted and evolve into a full-blown siege. Of course, the basis of each is the same – someone holed up in a house or flat refusing to comply or let the police in, but this is where the similarity ends. The important part is why it has happened, and this is where things start getting complicated as there could be myriad reasons.

For a response sergeant, these incidents can be high risk and also resource intensive, but anyone worth their salt wants to be involved in them; they are what you join the job for. More often than not, there is a moment very early on in proceedings where, if the officers act quickly and decisively, they can stop the incident before it even starts. Sounds easy!

Fortunately, it wasn't long after I had qualified as a hostage and crisis negotiator that I got my eagerly awaited chance to test out my newfound skills in the art of communication.

The benefit of being on a response team is that you are readily available and, to be blunt, you also have means to get there in a hurry.

I was the duty sergeant working a late shift when a call came in about a disturbance at a block of flats. It sounded like a pretty routine job, a bit of shouting and banging coming from a top-floor flat, so officers were dispatched to investigate.

On their arrival they made their way to the third floor and could hear quite a commotion coming from inside. A short time later the occupant made himself known to them by throwing what seemed to be the entire contents of his flat out of the front window.

It was clear that this was not going to be one of those occasions for quick, decisive action.

On my arrival I parked a short distance back and began to walk towards the block. I could hear the man shouting, as the windows of the flat were open, and, as I got closer, I could see the splintered and smashed furniture lying in the car park below. It looked like there was a chest of drawers, maybe a table and a fair amount of glass.

I was there to negotiate with the man and hopefully help to resolve the situation safely. Negotiators don't get a great write up from their colleagues as their presence generally means that there won't be action any time soon as we wait for them to bore the person into submission. It's not *quite* like that, and it's more art than science. The key thing is to remember that if the situation can be sorted out without any force being used and, most importantly, without anyone being hurt then that is a positive thing.

It appeared that things had deteriorated quite rapidly, and the officers remained outside the flat door, which was locked.

The man inside was manic; shouting over and over again and making all sorts of threats. He told the officers that he had a microwave behind the door and he had filled it with fertiliser and he would blow the flat up. That was a major concern and promptly necessitated the entire block being evacuated – the last thing we wanted was mass casualties or even fatalities. He was also shouting that he would go and get a gun. The stakes were high.

I remained outside, straining my neck to look up at the window above us. I was joined by another negotiator named Andrew and we started to come up with a plan. I was eager to take on the role of lead negotiator, but my colleague was considerably more experienced and he took that job. I remember feeling relief that I would be playing the support role.

So, we got under way. Andrew called up to the man in the flat and after a few moments he appeared at the window – I have already mentioned first impressions and how important these can be to a negotiation.

It's fair to say that initial interactions with very angry individuals generally don't go well, and this was no different.

'Why don't you just fuck off?' he yelled.

Well, that told us then. Andrew was a very straight-talking, normal bloke and was always good at developing a rapport, so I was confident that after that initial blip we'd be in business fairly soon.

I was right. The man came back to the window regularly and would engage in some dialogue, before returning to the front door to shout at the officers and make a few more threats.

The man seemed very dismissive and certainly didn't want to talk about what the problem was.

'I don't need you here, you can go. You won't be able to help.' As I said earlier, these incidents are all pretty similar but for us, as negotiators, we want to know why today? Why now? What has happened that has meant that this man, who judging from his lack of police record seemed pretty rational, had suddenly found himself in this position?

If we can work that out then perhaps we can work out how to help him.

After around half an hour of Andrew shouting up at the window, we decided that we needed to move to the next phase of the game plan so my colleague went off to speak to our coordinator. The coordinator acts as a link between the negotiators and the tactical teams, whether that is firearms officers or riot cops.

This incident definitely warranted both as there was a clear risk to the officers at the door of the flat, so a steady stream of officers arrived with a van load of shields and protective kit.

While Andrew was away I remained nearby, hovering in the car park close to the window. I remember thinking how this felt just like our training; that's testament to the intensive course we had been through to qualify as negotiators.

I was hoping that the man would stay inside the flat and not engage with me out of the window before Andrew got back, not because I didn't want to speak to him but because it would just be simpler that way.

All of a sudden he came back to the window and shouted down to me, 'Andy, is that you?'

I guess I was about to get my first taste of negotiating. 'No, it's Ali. Andy has had to go and speak to someone. He'll be back in a minute.'

We had spent the majority of the first hour trying to persuade the man to give us his mobile number so we could speak to him on that. It's very difficult to have a sensible, meaningful conversation with someone when you are having to shout at the top of your voice.

Much to my surprise he told me to call him and he then proceeded to shout out his mobile number. I frantically looked around, hoping that Andrew would be back and could make the call, but I also didn't want to piss him off by not calling him. I decided to make the call.

Police officers are great at getting things done, generally quickly. Whether it's a domestic incident, a car crash or perhaps a crime report to be taken, we just get on with it. I think that comes with the job; you go from event to event to event and often you barely get time to eat let alone sit around and ponder what to do.

Officers are also great at offering people advice and giving them a hundred and one things to think about. That's the problem with situations like this, though, as no matter how much we think we know about the person or the predicament that they're in, we don't know as much as they do. I've heard it a thousand times and I've probably said it a few times too, 'What you need to do is . . .' The man in that flat was in crisis. Something had happened that had made him lose all rational thought, all self-control and, most importantly, all value for his life.

If there is one lesson to be learnt it is this: don't try and solve all their problems – they are their problems and they need to solve them. That may sound uncaring or even callous but it's not meant to be. What I have come to realise is that for someone to be so deep in crisis that they can see no way out, there must be something that has been consuming them. They will have spent every waking hour thinking about it so to come along and suddenly have all the answers is just not going to happen.

I dialled the number and gave the guy a call. Straight away we were able to start talking about what had happened and I was able to listen to him much more intently.

He was softly spoken and quite calm on the whole but from time to time he'd blast off again. This is pretty normal and understandable; he certainly didn't expect to be in this predicament when he got up that morning.

Over the course of the next few hours it became clear what the issue was and it was the bedroom tax. I'm sure that I could have spent all day writing down reasons why someone would lose the plot and that wouldn't have featured.

The bedroom tax was brought in during 2013 and it basically meant that if you lived in a housing association property, you'd get less housing benefit if you had a spare room. This guy had lived in his flat for a number of years but things had started to fall apart, he'd lost his job and now with the introduction of the bedroom tax he wouldn't be able to stay; he was going to lose his home.

I have never underestimated how important a home is to someone: it is their place of safety, their sanctuary from the outside world, and for him to be facing the prospect of losing it was simply too much for him to bear.

It also became really clear that this guy had something else on his mind, his daughter. Initially he was very reluctant to speak about her and that was absolutely fine. I was there to listen and I wanted to show him the respect and dignity he deserved, but after a short time he started to speak about her more and more.

He told me he was a terrible father. It was clear that he felt completely inadequate and yet he told me that when his daughter came to visit at the weekends, he would not eat from Friday morning until Monday because he couldn't afford to feed them both. Does that sound like a terrible father? That sounds like a situation that the vast majority of people couldn't even comprehend.

I felt that we were now talking man to man. I felt that he realised I wasn't there to judge him and importantly I wasn't there to make suggestion after suggestion of what he needed to be doing with his life to sort all this out; as I say, it's his problem to fix. But I was there to show him compassion and humanity and convince him that there was a light at the end of the tunnel and that he could turn things around, or at least he needed to try.

I thought we had made progress and he agreed to come out of the flat. He knew he would be arrested because I had told him that and he understood.

We talked about what would happen when he came out and he also said he understood that. He finished the call and made his way to the front door. I waited in the car park below, my heart beating fast and strong, hoping to hear that he was out safely and nobody had come to any harm.

All of a sudden there was an almighty noise from the landing of the flats and I could hear the man shouting aggressively.

I moved forward and with an approving nod from the coordinator I ran up to the top of the stairs, bounding up three steps at a time. As I got to the top landing, I could see the riot cops, wearing balaclavas and helmets stood at the door, with the man repeatedly kicking and punching their shields.

I pushed my way to the front and from just behind the riot shields I shouted his name to try and get his attention. 'I'm here, you're OK, talk to me.' I was frantically waving my arms trying to get his attention.

How had we gone from him being so calm to being so violent in such a short space of time? I shouted his name again but he was purely focused on the shields and the officers holding them.

He then shouted, 'I'm going to count to five and then I'm going to do it, I'll jump out of the window and kill myself.'

And then he started the countdown. Five, four, three, two and then he turned and ran into the flat. The shields froze and held their ground at the door.

I ran back downstairs fully expecting to see or hear him fall. Much to my relief he hadn't jumped but that relief was short lived.

The man had climbed out of the window and was now stood, precariously balancing on the window ledge. He was leaning forward, away from the window, just holding on with one hand and he was angry.

He was shouting my name over and over again, 'Ali, you've done this. Tell my daughter that you killed her daddy.'

I was shouting, 'Don't do it, please, please don't do it.'

He then began shouting to the onlookers who had gathered in the street to watch the incident unfolding and he addressed them directly, 'Make sure you tell them: "Ali did this." Tell my daughter he killed her daddy.'

I can't begin to describe the anguish and sheer terror that struck me but I had no time to dwell on it, I had to do all that I could to get him back to where we had been less than two minutes earlier.

I carried on shouting his name, desperately pleading with him not to do it. I then took a gamble, I asked him what I could do to stop him from jumping? I say it's a gamble because you just don't know what they are going to say and perhaps it would be something that I just couldn't deliver. I felt that the stakes were so high that I needed to do something and, as always, it's better to try and fail than not to try at all.

The man shouted down to me that he would go back inside the flat if I came up and saw him, but it had to be just me. In almost any other circumstance this would have been an absolute no, but as negotiators we never say never and this is a good example of why.

I turned to the coordinator and, without uttering a word, asked the question. The reply was prompt and was that it was up to me. I ran towards the communal door, shouting at the man to just wait, I was coming.

For the second time I bounded up the stairs and this time the front door was clear of riot police who had all moved back.

I opened the front door and called the man's name, 'I'm here, I'm coming inside.'

I stepped into the hallway and heard the door close behind me. This was the same man who had been threatening to blow up his flat earlier, who had said he had a gun and who had been fighting with the shields, but strangely I trusted him. Of course, there was a chance that he wanted me to come inside the flat so he could harm me, but I felt not.

I walked down the hallway and entered the front room. He was now straddling the window ledge and he turned to look over his shoulder.

'It's Ali, you can come back inside now,' I said. He immediately began to climb back through the open window to safety.

My heart felt like it was beating out of my chest but within a few seconds he was sat on his sofa.

He began sobbing, crying uncontrollably. I sat down next to him, put my arm around his shoulder and offered what reassurance I could. I felt absolutely drained.

'What happens to me now?' he asked.

'You're going to have to be arrested.' I wanted him to remember that this is the low point, from here on he could start looking to the future, with his daughter.

'Will you arrest me, Ali? I want you to do it.'

That isn't what happens, as negotiators don't arrest people, it's just not what we do. I told the man, 'I really don't want to do that. I'm here to help you, not arrest you.' I told him it would be someone else.

He turned to me, tears streaming down his cheeks and still with my arm round his shoulder. 'Please will you arrest me, Ali? I trust you.' What a strange world we live in.

After the incident I went back to the police station and wrote up my statement and notes. I wanted to make it clear in my arrest statement that this man needed help, he needed support and he most definitely did not need to go to prison.

I had spent several hours of my life speaking to him about things that were very personal to him, and it was clear that he was a proud, honest, hard-working guy who had fallen on hard times and was struggling to cope.

It couldn't be ignored that he threatened to blow up his flat, he had damaged property and he had tied up countless police resources over many, many hours, but I desperately hoped that the court would show him some compassion and leniency.

I was delighted to hear from his solicitor that he had been to court and that my statement had been of significance and he didn't go to prison. I've never seen or heard from the man again but I genuinely hope that things are better for him now.

20

Give me some advice

THE ROLE OF a tactical advisor sounds straightforward, but in reality it is anything but. Tactical advisors, or 'tac ads' as they are also known, are there to support commanders when dealing with the most serious incidents. The two most common types are in firearms and public order.

The concept is that you are there to be the sounding board and conscience of the commander while also having a detailed knowledge of tactics and legislation. In 2012 I became a public order tac ad and it's a role that I thoroughly enjoyed. In later years I also became a nationally accredited command trainer so I had the honour of training public order commanders and also future tactical advisors.

When explaining the role I would refer to a plane crash that took place in 1999; a Korean cargo plane crashed soon after taking off from Stansted. The plane was being flown by a former colonel of the Korean military and the first officer was a very young, inexperienced airman.

When the black box data was reviewed and the air accident investigation completed, it became clear that the pilot had been banking the plane to the left and had basically flown it into the ground, killing all four crew on board. What was also interesting was that despite the instruments clearly showing the first officer what was happening and a warning alarm sounding, he said nothing to challenge his far more experienced colleague. Why? Why would he not have been shouting at the pilot to change their course? We will never know for sure but perhaps it was because he felt unable to, or that it was just not the done thing to challenge someone who was, in his eyes, superior.

There were also elements of this in the worst aviation disaster in history: a crash in 1977 where a KLM jet and a Pan Am jet collided on the runway in Tenerife. As the captain of the KLM plane opened the throttles, the first officer asked whether they were clear for take off. He was not insistent when challenging his more senior colleague, but he was clearly in some doubt because he asked the question in the first place. Perhaps he felt unable to push the point any further. The crash resulted in 583 people being killed.

These theories make sense and they are compelling reasons as to why the UK use tactical advisors as they do. The tactical advisors are there to push the point, challenge commanders and ask the difficult questions irrespective of how uncomfortable that may feel for all involved.

I must make it clear: commanders command and advisors advise. Some people think that is not the case and commanders will acquiesce to the advice they receive. That is certainly not my experience over the years and rightly so.

I was in a slightly more unusual position because I would also train the commanders so they may have felt that to take my advice was the safest option but that would be poor leadership. I would always make it very clear at the start of an operation: I was there to give options and advice outlining the benefits and challenges, and then the commander would make the ultimate decision.

The other striking thing that I noticed was how lonely a position it is for the commanders; they earn the big bucks but they also make the big decisions and they know that their actions may be scrutinised in the cold light of day for years to come.

Giving advice is a bit of an art. The information and advice needs to be sufficient to help make some decisions, but it can't be *War and Peace* – we'd be there all day and policing operations are often dynamic.

I must say that the commanders I worked with in Suffolk were brilliant; thoroughly kind, decent senior officers who were very, very good at what they did. And they just got it. There was no arrogance and the first person they would ask for on a big job would be a tac ad, and that wasn't so they had someone to make the tea!

I think it's fair to say that all tac ads would have their own preferred option in mind when they were giving advice but it's not their decision, they are just the advisors.

The only caveat I'd put on that is that if the decision being made by the commander is dangerous and will put people's lives at risk or show complete disregard for legislation, then it was my job to tell them that and to push the point. I'd normally start with some verbal advice and discuss it. If it was still falling on deaf ears and time allowed then I'd commit it to paper and provide formal written advice. This was always a very good way to present the advice as it ensured that there were no misunderstandings and the commander understood the information and the implications.

One commander during a training course once said that by doing that a tac ad is twisting the commander's arm up their back. Not at all. If they still don't agree with the written advice then they would have to write up their own rationale as to why, or perhaps get some legal counsel. In my experience it never got to that stage but it shows that rank is irrelevant, it's all about role.

A particular incident that I remember as a tac ad was one of the worst outbreaks of disorder in Suffolk. In December 2016 a double murder took place on West Meadows travellers' site just outside Ipswich. The site was well established and somewhere I knew well, and on the whole it was settled and we had very few issues.

After the murders the site was thrown into a state of high tension; you could feel it as soon as you went through the gates. I had been on a counterterrorism negotiators' course in Norwich and had been summoned back on the day of the murders to help with the policing response.

As soon as I arrived it was clear that this was a highly sensitive operation. It would be vital that the murder investigation could be completed while the public order commanders ensured that there was no further violence or disorder on the site. Easier said than done.

After roughly three days, the site remained very tense and officers were permanently deployed there to ensure the murder scenes were preserved so the forensic examinations could take place.

I had worked on the case since the start and having done a whole day's planning I handed over to a colleague in the evening, when myself and the Silver Commander stood down. We felt that we had a good plan for the week ahead and we left it in the safe hands of the late-turn chief inspector.

At around 10 p.m. I was just driving along the A14 heading home when I received a call from the tac ad on lates. She shouted down the phone, 'They're torching the site, they're setting it on fire.'

By the time she stopped saying this I could already see the billowing smoke from the site as the night sky turned orange. I was only a few minutes away from Ipswich Police Station so I headed straight there. You may be wondering why we didn't all head straight to the scene. It's almost impossible to command an incident like this, at a tactical level, if you're there on the ground. Many a commander over the years will have been tempted to get too close and in doing so will have lost all oversight of the operation. A good analogy is that to win a game of chess, you need to see the whole board and you can't do that if you're one of the pieces.

This was going to prove to be one of the most challenging nights of my career.

The Silver Commander is responsible for the tactical plan – they basically outline the tactics and the officers on the ground deliver them under the direction of the Bronze Commander. It's a bit like football. The manager who picks the team and sets the tactics is the Silver Commander and the captain who leads the players on the pitch is the Bronze Commander.

As soon as the Silver Commander had arrived at the police station all hell had broken loose. The caravan that had been part of the crime scene had been torched, and the officers had been threatened and told to get off the site by men with axes and weapons.

Due to the resourcing implications of the murder investigation we already had colleagues from across the region supporting us and it had been some unfortunate Bedfordshire officers who had been told to leave in no uncertain terms. I remember hearing one of them say, 'And I thought Luton was rough!' as he arrived back at the police station.

The next few hours were like a game of Top Trumps with every one of the updates relaying yet another threat to life.

The Silver Commander had assembled his team in the control suite and it included a senior detective from the investigation team for the murders, specialist operations staff, intelligence officers, a fire officer, an ambulance officer and a representative from the press office.

The first problem that we had was that the burning caravan could not be extinguished as the steam from the fire would have struck the overhead national grid cables and would have electrocuted anyone nearby.

The group behind the incident then stole a small van from the site and began driving it round and round, smashing into other vehicles and caravans. They then began smashing up a caravan and appeared to be preparing to set light to it; the main problem was that there was a gas tank at the back of it. I remember asking the fire officer, 'Presumably you mean a gas cylinder?'

'No, I mean a gas tank with a four-hundred-metre exclusion zone around it!' he clarified.

'Ah right, OK!'

All the time that this was going on cops were waiting at the entrance to the site, desperately hoping that the resources that were now on their way from all over the south-east and London would just hurry up and get there.

In the Silver Suite it was clear that the stakes were high and the Silver Commander told the room that he feared that someone would die on the site and it might be a member of the public or a police officer.

Everyone was well aware of that but when you hear those words it makes you realise: this is real and this is as serious as it gets. There could be an explosion, the stolen van could run someone over or the other residents on the site could take matters into their own hands.

As the tac ad, I was continually being asked for advice about tactics and the capabilities of the resources we had. Did we have enough? Could we get back on to the site? Unfortunately, the answer was no, not in my opinion. Everyone has a right to life and that includes the cops, and to put them on the site would have put their lives in grave danger.

As the night wore on the disorder continued and we were continually being updated by the air observer in the police helicopter. They hovered for hours over the site, keeping tabs on the main offenders and filming the destruction taking place.

After a while the offenders dumped the van and went to the field at the back of the site. There they found a horse tethered to the ground and they set about attacking it with bits of wood and axes. The air observer was understandably distressed by what they were seeing; it was clear for everyone to hear.

'They are attacking the animal, it can't get away, it's tethered to the ground.' They were urging the Silver Commander to get resources on the site.

This seemed to take matters to a whole new level and everyone in the Silver Suite listened in amazement at the abhorrent barbarism of what was happening.

At the beginning of the night the suite had been a busy, bustling place but as the severity of what was happening grew in intensity, and lives became ever more at risk, it became quieter and quieter until only those who absolutely had something to say would speak.

The Silver Commander, who had been pacing the room, turned to me and said, 'Tactical advisor, give me some advice.'

It's in moments like this that you realise giving advice is tough and although you're not the decision maker you don't want to let your colleagues down and you are under immense pressure to deliver. I felt strangely cold and disconnected from it all. It felt like a training exercise, the type that I'd so often put commanders and tactical advisors through as part of my role as a command trainer.

I said to the Silver Commander, 'If this was a tabletop exercise and an animal was being killed, what would you do? Would you go on or would you decide that as abhorrent as it is, it's animal cruelty and you wait for more resources?'

He agreed and the decision was made that the officers would not go in yet, as to do so would put everyone's life at risk.

I remember at that point thinking about why we do this job and what guides us when making such difficult decisions. The British model of policing is one centred around consent. What would the public expect us to do?

I looked across the room at the press officer who had been listening intently throughout the night. She was relatively new to the organisation and she was as close as we'd get to a member of the public; I wondered what she thought and what her take on it was. At the end of the day, if someone died it would be twelve decent men and women judging our actions in a Coroner's Court so it was important that we always kept that principle in mind.

A short time later more officers arrived and the Bronze Commander on the ground had a plan, was ready and they entered the site. Lines of cops and ferocious dogs began roaming around the site and the offenders starburst in every direction, jumping fences, hiding in caravans and even running across the dual carriageway in an attempt to evade the police.

After some excellent work by the crew in the police helicopter all the main offenders were arrested. A vet attended to the horse but unfortunately its life was already lost; a tragic stain on the night's disorder.

Some parts of the site had been totally destroyed: broken glass strewn across the roadways, smashed fences, wrecked caravans and a written-off van. The damage would run into tens of thousands of pounds but nobody had been killed.

When the officers came back to the nick some of them were furious; 'It's a fucking disgrace,' I heard one of them say.

'What a complete joke,' another one remarked. 'Why were we not given the green light to enter the site when the horse was being attacked?'

That's one of the big decisions that had to be taken and that's why it's a lonely place for the commanders, but when the emotion is taken out of it all, it was absolutely the right decision to make.

The following day we returned to work for another late shift, and now the site was calm and the tension had reduced. It was almost as though the steam had come out of it and the site was in a far better place than twenty-four hours earlier.

I took the chance to watch the footage from the police helicopter. It was incredibly powerful, particularly when the horse was killed. A group of men, armed with axes and pieces of wood, slaying a poor defenceless animal. The horse dropped to its knees and gradually its life slipped away. I can see why the crew in the helicopter were so distressed by it. Did I think the commander had made the wrong decision and that he should have sent the police officers in at that point? No, absolutely not.

It is an incident that I will never forget as it showed how unpredictable policing is and it showed that all the training we do, particularly with the commanders, pays off when it really matters. I have the utmost respect for all the commanders who put themselves in positions such as these and the tac ads who make such valuable contributions.

For me personally this was a traumatic and truly difficult incident and it remained on my mind for long periods of time. I will never be able to drive past the site and not think back to how fortunate we were to have the right people in charge that night, holding their nerve and keeping everyone safe.

In total I worked nearly twenty night shifts in a row during a really tough time and it seemed that no sooner than this incident had been resolved, Ipswich descended into a period of violent crime the likes of which we'd never encountered before.

21

Hitting rock bottom

FOR THE NEXT three months my colleagues and I in central Ipswich felt we were fighting a tide of violence. There were murders, stabbings, muggings, robberies, attacks on officers and, on top of this, a seething frustration and anger often directed at the police.

I was very aware of the pressure of public expectation. They looked to us to keep them safe and this was proving to be increasingly difficult. Barely a day would go by without the media highlighting a significant event or incident and it felt very much that this was done with an accusatory tone; almost questioning what on earth we were doing about it.

I'm sure that most police officers feel the same when I say that you take it personally. It feels like you are failing, even if it's not your fault. It feels like you are letting people down. I was a sergeant and I could see the effect it was having on some of the most resilient, battle-hardened cops I'd ever worked with.

I'd experienced many occasions in my career where demand would surge and it felt like you were holding on for dear life, but this seemed different. I'd not known it to be so fast paced and working on an emergency response team you felt it more than most.

I remember one night in February 2017 where we attended the scene of a stabbing. The incident was near to the main Ipswich railway station. We weaved our way through the busy rush-hour traffic, sirens screaming and the blue lights rebounding off the buildings.

My colleague and I arrived moments after the call came in, jumping out of our police car, which I'd abandoned at the side of the road. We rushed over to a man who was lying on the pavement at the side of the carriageway. We'd arrived at the same time as the paramedic, who ran to the back of his car to get his medical kit. The man had been stabbed in the chest. He was still alive but he'd been fatally wounded, and died a short time later.

This incident alone stretched the team and the force to the absolute limit but the emergency calls just kept coming. While I was standing at the scene of the murder, call after call after call just kept coming over the police radio. It was going to be a long, relentless night.

Almost without me realising, this started to chip away at my mental health. At the time, I was living in the moment, simply surviving from one hour to the next, one shift to the next, one month to the next. There were days when I'd get up, go to work, go home to sleep and then go back to work. It was quite literally a revolving door and I was just waiting for my days off to recover.

Things came to a head in March 2018 when I suddenly found myself spiralling out of control. In short, I suffered a serious mental breakdown. No longer was I surviving.

To say it was the scariest time of my life would be an understatement – mentally broken, unable to control my emotions, gripped with anxiety and heading to rock bottom.

It's strange how, looking back now, one of my closest friends had said to me the week before, 'You're a man on the edge.' I dismissed it and felt he was being dramatic, but clearly he was right.

He was someone who I had known my whole career and he became my closest friend. He was my confidant, someone who I could go to for advice. Ironically, he was also someone who I often wouldn't agree with! He was very similar in terms of his work ethic and desire to be successful.

Some people found us an odd partnership; I recall my mum once saying, 'You're both very different!' She was, of course, right in many ways but we shared a lot of things in common too and he was always the first person I'd call in a crisis, which speaks volumes for how close we were.

In the days leading up to my breakdown it was almost as though all the instruments were telling me everything was OK, and despite a bit of turbulence I was maintaining height. In actual fact I was flying myself into the ground and, before I knew it, I had crashed. My friend, knowing me so well, could see it was going wrong in front of his very eyes.

Having finally broken, I'd regularly dream about killing myself or being murdered at work and yet I can assure you I had no intention of these events happening. It showed me how out of control my mind had become and if I could not control my thoughts then how could I be sure that I'd be able to control my actions? What if I lost control? What if I did something to hurt myself that I didn't want to do?

It was the sort of anxiety that leaves you terrified, pumped full of adrenaline, feeling physically unwell and unable to face the world.

Things finally came to a head when I travelled to the north-west with two work colleagues to observe a football operation. I'd been feeling stressed and under pressure, but that was pretty normal for me and I remember really looking forward to it. I was well used to travelling and I enjoyed the company of the colleagues I was going with. I had no idea what was about to happen.

On our arrival at the hotel in Manchester I felt an overwhelming sense of anxiety coming over me. It was as though I was becoming detached from reality and everything was crashing down around me.

As I checked in, I could barely hear what the lady on reception was saying to me and it was as though I wasn't really present. I grabbed the paperwork and key off the desk and got in the lift with my colleagues.

As soon as I got into my room I crashed and burned in spectacular fashion. I stood in my hotel room on the seventh floor, looking across the city, and felt completely alone and overwhelmed.

I remember it as though it was yesterday – a lost soul in a big city. I just had to get out of there and, before I knew it, I was boarding a train and heading to London, leaving all my belongings and my colleagues behind. Why London? It was generally in the direction of home and it was the first train that I could get from the station.

I almost didn't care where I was going, I just had to get out of there.

I found a spare seat on the train and slumped into it. I sat with tears silently streaming down my cheeks and unable to function.

I was a complete mess and totally broken. I remember looking around the carriage and wishing I was like the other people on the train, seemingly happy, carefree and enjoying life.

Thinking about it now, despite the state I was in, not one person on that train asked me if I was OK or even offered me a reassuring smile – the world seemed a pretty dark place.

My best friend came to pick me up from London. He was the very same friend who had seen the warning signs the week before and now he was about to see the reality of it.

I stood outside the station in the pouring rain, desperately wanting to see his car come around the corner. He called me. 'I'm parked outside, where are you?'

I walked the short distance to his car and got in. We barely spoke on the way back. I just sat with tears in my eyes, exhausted and empty.

Little did I know that my life was going to get as tough as it had ever been. I got home late that night and quickly hurried into my house, locking the doors and battening down the hatches. It felt like a sanctuary compared to the big city and it felt like, for now at least, I'd be safe.

In the following days I tried to get some help as my mind and thoughts were out of control. I was waking up and my heart rate was racing at over 120 beats a minute. I was having nightmares every time I slept, which wasn't often. I couldn't stop breaking down and I lost any ability to look after myself. I didn't eat for five days and normal everyday tasks had become simply impossible. It felt like I was in a permanent state of red alert; it was as though I was sitting stationary in my car in first gear, with the clutch down but my foot was flat on the accelerator. The engine, my mind, was revving at full throttle and not surprisingly it had just blown up.

I called my GP first thing in the morning to be told they had no appointments and I needed to call back the following day. The following day! I wasn't even sure if I'd last that long.

I couldn't eat, I couldn't sleep and I certainly couldn't think. I had been desperately waiting to call the doctor, in the hope that they would look after me and make this excruciating anxiety disappear. Fortunately, I've got some amazing friends and family, the type of people who would drop anything and be there in a flash, the type of people who you need in a crisis.

That afternoon, in a state of desperation I called the force employee assistance service and spoke to a counsellor on the phone for an hour. He was a young Scottish guy and he was amazing – kind, reassuring, compassionate and completely non-judgemental. He just listened, as simple as that. It's the strangest of concepts that a fellow human being, whom I have never met and probably never will, can reach out and somehow make your darkest hour slightly better.

I have no idea who he was or even his name but if you ever read this, thank you.

My closest friends would text me often, offering to come round or give me a call. It helped just knowing that they were there. Importantly, they weren't too intrusive; I wanted things to be on my terms. There was nothing that they could say or do to make things better.

My family, meanwhile, were still a little in the dark in terms of just how poorly I was, but they will have realised that things were not great.

It felt really surreal trying to get help. I was a police sergeant and the one who people turned to when they were in trouble. When everyone would be taking a step back or turning the other cheek, I'd be stepping forward, offering a hand and sorting things out. Throughout my service I'd been a 'go to' person who'd help take care of others; I'd even occasionally get calls from hardened criminals who had found themselves in trouble and they were turning to me to help them. All of a sudden I was the one who needed help.

Our team were told that I was going to be off work for a while and that they were not to contact me. I'd spoken to one of the commanders at Ipswich and we'd decided that would be best. No details. They were told that any queries had to go through the Inspector. Why did I think that was the right thing to do? Over the years that had almost become the default way in the police. If anyone ever told me they were suffering in the way that I was I'd be completely supportive, so why did I feel that I needed to hide the reason I was off? People were rarely, if ever, told that someone was suffering with a mental health problem. It's strange now I think back because everyone found out eventually, but it just meant that there would be weeks of rumours.

I decided to send the team a message and explain exactly what had happened; it was sincere, heartfelt and completely honest.

> I hope that you're all well. I wanted to send you a message to let you know what has happened. I have had a complete mental breakdown. I know that you were not told very much other than that you were not to contact me but I want to be honest with you. How can I expect other people to be honest when they are struggling if I can't do that myself? I don't know how long I will be off but I don't think I will be back any time soon. I will be back in touch when I am ready but please take care of each other.

The responses were predictable: supportive, compassionate and kind. That initial lack of honesty is the stigma that still exists.

If I had been involved in a serious car accident and was going to be off work for a while, everyone would be told that, but because I had suffered a mental breakdown, that needed to be kept out of the public domain.

If anyone reading this is unfortunate enough to find themselves in this position then my advice would be to be honest and you'll be amazed at how kind and supportive people will be.

It's not just the police, though. For almost a year the vast majority of my friends outside of the police were blissfully unaware that I was not only off work but that I was really poorly. Clearly, it's a personal decision to tell people but I found not being honest truly exhausting and it felt like I was living a lie. I'd forget who knew and who didn't, and my very existence became a constant charade.

My family were unsure what to tell people; again, this shows the difference between mental and physical health. If I was off work with a broken leg, we wouldn't be discussing what we should tell people. It also meant that I had to cope with constantly being asked about work as everyone seems to be fascinated with policing. If I had my time again, I'd have been more honest across the board and I think that would have helped me greatly.

Having opened up about my experiences I have been staggered at just how many people have either suffered themselves or know someone close to them who has. It is perhaps this more than anything else that makes me realise just how good we are at keeping this out of the public eye. I have found the countless messages of support and encouragement truly humbling. Too many people are suffering in silence and by doing so are cutting off so much support.

I would liken it to the positive steps we've made in society in relation to the LGBT community. It is a personal decision whether to come out or not, or how much of our personal lives we share with friends, colleagues and strangers. But nobody should feel that they can't be honest about their own situation through fear of ridicule or derision.

I hope that, in years to come, our mental health comes to be regarded in the same way as everything else that makes each and every one of us who we are.

After a couple of days I managed to find a consultant psychologist and I visited him early one Monday morning, desperately hoping that he would be able to fix me.

I wasn't completely sure what to expect – I sat in the waiting room, trembling and on the verge of breaking down again. It was a strange sensation, not so much anticipation or even apprehension, perhaps just resignation.

As Dr Syd Hiskey walked in to get me from the waiting room, I could barely hold myself together, but we slowly climbed the spiral staircase to his room.

We talked quietly for an hour about what had happened and how I was now unable to cope. I was not very talkative so he had to drag it out of me, piece by piece.

At the end of the session he told me what he thought the issue was.

'Ali, from what you've told me, some people may say that you're suffering with work-related stress.' He then carried on, 'You're actually showing symptoms of complex post-traumatic stress disorder, depression and severe anxiety.'

He asked me how I felt about that, and I replied that I didn't feel anything; I just felt numb. The words didn't mean a great deal at that time.

He prepared me for a long road ahead. He said it may take many, many months and he couldn't guarantee that I'd improve let alone make a full recovery.

He seemed taken aback at my mental state and how severe my symptoms were, and he explained just how bad it was.

Syd also explained how he would normally see people around eight or ten times and he hoped by then they would have made real progress. He went on, 'There are some who won't make any progress at all.'

The words reverberated around my mind. He paused, hesitated slightly and told me that he might see me between twenty-four and thirty-six times and I might make no progress at all. I slumped in my chair, shattered, scared and speechless.

When I left the room, I was mentally on my knees. I remember reading somewhere that depression is like an ocean compared to sadness, which is like a raindrop. I recall thinking, 'That's a bit dramatic,' and yet here I was out of my depth and being swept out to sea, totally paralysed by fear and anxiety, unable to swim and barely able to keep my head above water. And they're right, the two are not comparable.

I'd never had a day's sickness in almost two decades of service and now I faced the prospect of being permanently damaged by the things I'd seen and done all in the name of public service. I had hit rock bottom.

22

A long road back

As the weeks passed I began to feel slightly more in control but the nightmares and uncontrollable panic attacks persisted, catastrophising what could happen and leaving me seemingly unable to cope with normal life let alone work.

One of my greatest strengths had always been my judgement, sense of perspective and decision making. Now it seemed that these attributes had been obliterated and my rational mind had become gripped with fear and paranoia. I'd have bad days and I'd have worse days, often for no apparent reason. My mind would fill with intrusive thoughts and I'd be unable to regain my composure for hours or even days.

I'd always been told that when you're suffering with mental ill health it's important to stay active and force yourself to get up and get on with life. That may work in some situations but it perhaps isn't as simple as that.

A colleague and dear friend who had been through a similar experience put me right – if you're having a bad day, don't fight it, accept it. Lie in bed, watch TV, eat what you want, spend some money, rest and, whatever you do, don't beat yourself up. If you were physically unwell you wouldn't force yourself out of bed, you'd take it easy, be kind to yourself and allow yourself to recover. And most importantly, remember that the next day will hopefully be better.

He was right: all of a sudden my bad days were not such an ordeal and invariably the following day would be a little better, and no longer would I find myself fighting my own mind to do things.

Importantly, I had to share this with my well-intentioned friends who would have to put up with me cancelling on them at short notice or turning up late. Rather than try and motivate me to get out, I needed them to just support me and not beat me up about it. It doesn't work the other way around, though! I'd often only feel up to doing one thing each day – maybe going to the shops or meeting a friend for a coffee or some food. If those plans got cancelled, it would leave me drifting for hours and invariably would result in me going back to bed.

My friends were great and rarely, if ever, let me down, which gave me the motivation to get up and get out, but don't ever underestimate how important those everyday things are to someone who is suffering.

As part of the work with the consultant I had to list all the triggers for my PTSD and anxiety. There were nearly forty initially and that gradually rose to over fifty – places, people, hearing about certain things, cars, criminals, colours, numbers, words and even items of clothing, and they all varied in severity.

Ironically for a response police officer of almost twenty years, seeing cops or even hearing sirens became an emotional ordeal. I had worked with a lot of officers over the years and some of them were now triggers – that included their epaulette numbers.

Their numbers would feature in number plates, phone numbers, house numbers – they seemed to be everywhere.

These triggers would result in me being flooded with adrenaline with my heart racing and feeling physically sick. The most severe triggers would cause me anxiety not for hours but for days or even weeks so I lived in fear of being triggered, knowing what would follow. For months I had to sleep with all the lights on as I felt so anxious; I even bought my first night light at the age of thirty-five!

I would be constantly on edge and expecting the worst, looking for dangers and completely paranoid. I'd travel miles and miles in my car so I didn't have to drive past certain locations and could avoid those things that made me feel so physically unwell as my mind would race at a million miles an hour. I'd convince myself that I was being followed or people were conspiring against me. If I saw someone in public take a phone call I'd spend hours totally convinced that it was about me. I felt like my life was at risk all day every day.

There would be entire weeks where I'd not be able to open my curtains as I just wanted to be cut off from the outside world and I was petrified that people would come to my house. I even changed my mobile number because every time it rang I would jump out of my skin and it could derail me for hours.

For a number of months I stopped reading the news as it was something I couldn't control and it could trigger me all over again. It was utterly exhausting.

The irony, though, is that the uncontrollable anxiety is the mind doing exactly what it's hardwired to do – keeping us alive. If at the end of the day you're curled up on the floor, consumed with anxiety and feeling awful, your mind doesn't care about that because it's achieved the objective of keeping you alive.

It was as though, as soon as the watch tower in my mind saw something approaching that it didn't like the look of, it would immediately hit the panic alarm. Knowing this was strangely useful as it went some way to explaining why these triggers were causing such an involuntary physical reaction. But it didn't take away from the fact that my life was a mess. It was like it wasn't really happening to me, but trust me, it was.

Working with my consultant, we gradually started to make sense of what was happening in my mind and he set me off on a course of therapy that revolved around compassion. I walked out of the first few sessions a little sceptical. Compassion-focused therapy? Is that really going to help me? Ultimately, yes! I can say this without hesitation. It calms your mind and helps you feel less threatened and anxious. It makes perfect sense; when a child cries they are soothed by the reassuring, kind and compassionate parent who holds them close, quietly telling them that they will be OK.

My consultant's knowledge and expertise were never in doubt but his caring, professional and supportive manner was equal in measure.

I also owe my friends and family a huge debt of gratitude. We embarked on a journey that none of us fully understood, but the phone calls, texts and visits gave me the drive to push on and try and fix this, but at my own pace, without judgement or pressure. A reassuring hand on the shoulder, a hug or shake of the hand can make all the difference.

I remember one day bumping into a defence solicitor who I'd known throughout my service. She had often sat on the other side of the court room or interview desk. As she walked past me in the street she smiled and quietly asked, 'Are you deep undercover today?'

On the spur of the moment I said to her, 'I guess that you've not heard. I'm off work at the moment. Things are not good.'

She paused, and we had a short chat. As we were about to go our separate ways she said to me, 'Remember you're one of the good ones; you're an honest hard-working man, so look after yourself.'

She will not have realised how important that bit of compassion was, but it turned a bad day into a far more positive one and it's something that I'll always be grateful for.

I also realised quite quickly how unforgiving we are to ourselves. I'd often tell myself to 'get a grip', 'pull yourself together' and 'what is the matter with you?!'

My consultant asked me a bit more about that. He gave me the example that someone from the team came to see me, they were tearful, frightened and gripped with anxiety. He asked me what I'd say to them.

I said I'd put my arm round their shoulder and I'd quietly tell them they were going to be OK and that I'd look after them. I'd tell them I was there for them and the whole team were there for them, that they weren't on their own. It's interesting. We often show unwavering compassion to others but we're perhaps not so kind to ourselves so be careful how you talk to yourself.

During my time off an old work friend contacted me out of the blue and invited me to pop round and see him. We spent hours talking, and he asked me what I thought was going on. 'I don't know, I'm struggling to make sense of it,' I replied.

'Well,' he said, 'I have some idea of how you're feeling. You're getting your world map and your territory mixed up.'

'What do you mean?' I asked.

'OK – this is how I see it,' he said. 'We've all got our own individual map of the world – influenced by what we've experienced, our upbringing, our relationships and, importantly for the police, our work. But our maps are never the same as the territory – that is reality. Imagine that your map is your personal outlook on life, whereas your territory is the same for all of us and it's the reality of where we live and what the world is really like.'

I thought about what he was saying. It made sense.

'So being a police officer – and seeing the things I have seen – has distorted my "map" and made it bleak, with people doing bad things in a bad world with very little light?'

'Yes, Ali, that's right. And what you need to remember is that your map is different to your territory – your reality. Because, in reality, most people are decent folks.'

Suddenly I had a moment of clarity. I could see that I had been looking at life through a distorted lens; filtering out the positive and just paying attention to all the bad stuff. I guess that was what had made me pretty effective as a cop over the years. But now I needed to redraw my own map.

I knew that in reality the vast majority of people would give you the shirt off their back if you needed it – though most of the time they just don't show it. Realising that my map was not the territory – and that I could redraw my map – was a key moment in my journey.

During this chapter in my life, what also became very clear very quickly was that everyone is different and as such every road to recovery will be unique. One size doesn't fit all when it comes to mental health – it's not like a broken arm that will take six weeks in a cast.

What I found was that I needed a plan and something to work towards in small, manageable steps, as I felt I was frozen in time and my life had literally stopped. To that end, I think I made a pretty significant mistake.

I had always had an insatiable work ethic and that drove me to work flat out in the highest pressure environments for almost two decades. Once I became poorly and I was off work, I replaced my drive for policing with my drive to recover.

It took over my life – matrixes of triggers, scales, journals, diagrams, meetings, counselling sessions. It became my full-time job but unlike policing it consumed me every single minute of every day and I couldn't clock off or go on rest days.

High drive can suppress the threat and anxiety that you feel but when the drive stops, which it will, you're back where you started from. I can imagine that the mental health experts and doctors who have helped me have found me fairly demanding at times!

I was determined to recover but I wanted to recover in double quick time, and better than anyone else. I wanted to get back to the job that I loved and excelled at. Failure was not an option and I'd do whatever it took to succeed.

My first week back at work was into a non-operational role at Police Headquarters. I was pretty chilled with it and thought it'd be a good place to start my gradual reintegration. Or perhaps not. It felt like I'd stepped on to a motorway and the cars were flying past me at 100 mph. I was completely overwhelmed and unable to cope.

I had to leave every day at lunchtime, sometimes having to build myself up just to drive home because I felt so physically unwell with anxiety; I just had to go to bed and sleep.

Prior to becoming unwell I never realised how much effect mental health would have on my physical wellbeing – headaches, pains, stomach cramps, insomnia, trembling, heart palpitations, fatigue, loss of appetite, restlessness, the list goes on and on.

How had I got to this point in my life where I could not cope with the simplest of jobs in the most supportive of environments?

Some really good advice I was given by a friend was that the reaction of colleagues would be patchy to say the least when I first got back to work. Some would see me coming and immediately turn around and walk the other way; some would act as though nothing had happened and barely acknowledge me; and others would walk over, shake my hand or give me a hug and say how good it was to see me back.

That advice was absolutely invaluable as I encountered all of those reactions in the first few hours.

I remember my very first encounter. I had literally just arrived at HQ and saw a colleague who loved to tell me what he was up to and how great a job he was doing! He's a thoroughly nice guy but someone who doesn't really listen to what you're saying as he's too busy talking. He saw me as I walked down a corridor and he looked like he'd seen a ghost. As he passed me, he said, 'All right,' and with that he was gone; it was like he had a train to catch.

As I carried on I smiled from ear to ear; this was what my friend meant. Either that or he did have a train to catch!

I don't blame the people who avoided me at all costs as they probably felt very uneasy about what to say, similar to when people return to work after a bereavement. Knowing what I know now, I'd definitely go over, give them a hug and let them know how good it was to see them back at work. Those reactions certainly helped me the most.

I'd also liken returning to work as a bit like trying to land a jumbo jet in the worst crosswind you can possibly imagine. It feels like you may not make it. As the plane gets closer and closer to the ground, it is being tossed around in the turbulent air with the pilot using all their skill to try to keep it under control. The passengers are desperately just wanting to get the tyres on the runway. As the rubber touches the tarmac, there is the inevitable twitch of the aircraft and a jolt but you're down, you've landed. It sounds terrifying and traumatic, and it was.

I'd never fully appreciated how hard returning to work would be.

After my first couple of weeks at HQ I decided to get in touch with the team again. I sent them a message.

> You're a top team and during tough times like the last week, you've got to stick together and get your heads down – there's no place for egos and attitudes and that's what the team has always been about. Work hard and just do your best.
>
> I think it's fair to say that I'm not coming back to the team and my mental health is still pretty fragile in relation to work. I'm at HQ and now I've landed there I reckon I'll not be operational for months.
>
> Take it from me, enjoy what you do because you never know when your playing days will be over and you could be a long time behind a desk! I'm always on the end of a phone so if you ever need anything then give me a bell.
>
> I've had my problems but I'm always happy to help others in any way I can. Take care of yourselves and keep fighting the good fight.

A couple of minutes later I got the first reply, 'Sound advice from the best.'

After a few months and having made my first attempt at getting back to operational work, it became clear that my mental health was more damaged than I had hoped. It resulted in a further period of sickness and a real recognition that one of my greatest strengths over the years, my resilience, had been shattered.

If it had just been broken then I'd have been able to quickly repair it by putting the bits back together, but it was shattered into a million pieces so the only option was to try and rebuild it all over again, and that takes time. It was also at this point that I realised that I'd just been driving my way through it by making my recovery my new full-time job.

While trying to come back to work, it also became apparent just how much I kept changing my mind. The once decisive decision-making machine was completely malfunctioning.

Some people were quite critical of that and I can understand just how frustrating it must have been for them, but rather than criticism I really needed support and understanding. It was a symptom of being so poorly.

A close friend of mine and I often reminisce now about just how erratic I had become – one day I was doing this, the next day I was doing that and then I'd end up back where I started. It was as exhausting for me as it was for the bosses trying to manage my return to work.

I remember one particular week when I was literally all over the place – I emailed my chief inspector on Monday to say that I was ready to get back to front-line duties and by the end of the week I was considering leaving the force!

Despite all of this I still had the same goal. I wanted to get back to operational policing. I wanted to experience the buzz of being a police officer, racing to attend incidents and making a real difference. It was all that I had ever known. I wanted to police again.

I spent many sleepless nights trying to comprehend what my life would be like without policing. In truth, I tried not to think about it too much as it made me feel even worse.

Policing is one of a handful of vocations that takes over your life in many ways – cops generally socialise with cops, your personal life is intrinsically linked to your occupation and it does, in many ways, define who you are. Many people will only ever have known me as Ali Livingstone, the police officer.

Having said all of that, I also knew that it was making me poorly – really poorly – and my life had become a never-ending ordeal. I'd always been very clinical in my decision making but this was different. Perhaps it was the mental illness, perhaps the emotion, or perhaps the enormity of it. In truth, why it was difficult was irrelevant; the fact remained, it was.

In the end the decision was almost made for me. I had a meeting with my inspector in December 2018 to discuss my return to my response team at Ipswich. I had walked into the meeting confident that we'd be able to get me back to work. We met in the canteen at Police Headquarters, a surprisingly common meeting place for these types of discussions. It was late afternoon, so we were the only people there.

I sat down opposite him and said, 'I'm ready to go back. I've completed all my refresher training, no problems, it's all gone to plan. I'm definitely ready.'

Over the previous weeks I'd been out several times with the response team to test myself out and although those shifts had been quite challenging for me, there had been no major hiccoughs.

I'd dealt with a few routine calls and even attended a suicidal male suffering a mental health crisis and it all felt normal, almost back to business.

I felt that I had to give it a go and continue to build on my recovery and push ahead. In no way was I certain I'd make it but, as I've said before, I'd rather try and fail than never try at all.

The Inspector was less than convinced. He looked uneasy, almost like he knew what he was going to say would not go down well with me.

'I just think that you're taking it too fast, Ali. I don't think you're ready yet.'

He clearly felt it may have been too soon, particularly as we'd had a false start some months earlier. I was not having that at all and I argued my point.

'I don't agree, I am really confident that I'll be fine once I am back there.' He wanted me to have a gradual, much slower reintroduction into the role and as the conversation went on I was becoming increasingly angry.

'What is wrong with you all? Why can't you see that I am ready?' I was enraged and on the verge of knocking him out! I stormed out of the meeting. 'I'm going on leave.'

I was furious that nobody seemed to understand or believe me when I said I was ready. I have never felt such anger and such a sense of injustice.

The following day I met one of my former bosses, Ben. For me, he was the perfect inspector; kind, caring, honest, funny and very straight talking. I loved working with him and the team absolutely adored him; they were without doubt the best years of my career and some of the best years of my life. If I had a problem or needed advice I'd go and see Ben.

We sat chatting about the meeting I'd had with my inspector the day before and I said to Ben, 'What is wrong with these people? Why can't they see I'm ready?'

Ben hesitated and then leant forward in his chair. He looked slightly uneasy as well, a little like my inspector had the day before.

'It's because you're not ready. I just don't think you're ready.'

I was stunned and speechless. I couldn't believe it. He was meant to be my friend and here he was telling me the same as everyone else! Slowly it dawned on me: what are they seeing that I'm not? Maybe I'm wrong and they are right. It was not a good place to be and it hit me really hard.

Over the next few weeks I went into a complete tailspin. No longer did I have the focus and drive to get back to work. I was now like a ship in a storm with no rudder, just being tossed and thrown around in the waves.

I struggled with sleep, having violent and distressing dreams most nights of terrorist incidents and police colleagues being beheaded; and uncontrollable bouts of depression and anxiety.

I would wake up in the morning and wish it was bedtime as that would mean I'd survived another day and I could tick it off on the calendar.

Perversely, when it did get to bedtime I'd dread falling asleep as I knew that I'd have yet more nightmares and when I did wake up it'd be the start of another day. I was not living life any more. I was just enduring it. I'd lock myself away and just lie in bed, often silently crying.

I would only be able to frequent locations I was familiar with, so travelling became an insurmountable problem. I'd have the sensation that my body was fizzing with anxiety as it trembled and shook, and I'd feel like I was not really present.

At times I felt broken beyond repair.

The realisation and acceptance that I was no longer fit to work in the life-and-death world of front-line policing was made harder because I'd convinced myself I was. I would liken it to a professional sportsman who is working towards a return and is convinced that their injured limb is strong enough and ready, only to be told that they are not fit and they may never be again.

My work had been the most significant part of my life; I fully committed to it and it was something that I loved. I loved the work itself, I loved the social element and I loved the camaraderie. Having had the realisation that I was now not going to be able to do the operational work that I loved so much, I had to make a decision: stay in the organisation and do something else or leave it all behind.

I thought long and hard about this. I had only ever been an operational officer; I had no interest in working a Monday to Friday administrative role. I joined the police for an all-action, life-at-risk, adrenaline-fuelled adventure and that is what I wanted to do.

If I could no longer do that then I'd rather leave.

The decision to leave was the one time during that part of my illness where I did really take my time. It was so important.

I considered lots of options; perhaps I should take a career break for a few years, as that would mean that I could go back to my old job once I felt better. That seemed logical but I started to realise that perhaps being a police officer was part of the problem and I needed a complete break. And maybe I had no intention of ever coming back because I could never see myself being well enough to be an operational cop again.

I also had the inevitable money worries. I had a mortgage to pay, a credit card and some car finance. I lived a good life, eating out, buying nice clothes; all things that had been funded by being a police sergeant. I was going to have to find a job that paid enough to make ends meet and my lifestyle might have to change.

In truth, when I was thinking this through, I didn't take a lot of advice. I was always fairly decisive when it came to making big calls and this was one of those occasions.

Health comes ahead of anything else and therefore leaving was the only choice and everything else would be a secondary consideration.

I was in the fortunate position that, having made the decision to go, I had plenty of time to find another job as I had over six months' worth of leave to use up first. I had built that up over the years, almost unwilling to take time off. In the end, it helped me greatly as I was still being paid while job hunting.

Having said all of that, when reality set in that I was actually leaving it felt like a bereavement; I felt like a complete failure and that I was letting a lot of people down.

The fact it was the 'right' decision didn't make it any easier. It left me feeling hopeless. It made me think about the work I'd done as a negotiator. When people are in crisis it is almost always because of a loss; the loss of their family, their work or their health are all examples.

I was now in that position and I'd lost my identity too.

I'd had eighteen years of full-on operational action and seen things I'd never wish on anyone, and I guess it had just taken its toll; I'd run out of gas and I'd lost my ability and desire to do it.

I'd spent my adult life at 100 miles per hour, kicking in doors, getting in fights, and I just couldn't do that all over again. Emotionally, physically and, most importantly, mentally, I was spent.

Many people over the years had warned me about burning out and I'd always laughed it off, 'I don't believe in all that rubbish.'

I guess for me it wasn't the long hours or the physically demanding nature of the job that had caught up with me, it was the pressure and mental element that had broken me.

Although I had been involved in a particularly traumatic event a few months earlier, I think that it became clear during my treatment that in fact I was suffering as a result of constant exposure to trauma and the threat-filled world in which I lived.

And when your trauma and anxiety are anchored to the job that you do, the job that defines you, eventually you have to decide what is in your own best interests, however hard that may be to accept.

The analogy that I use is that if I had been in a plane crash and survived, would I want to fly again? Probably not unless it was vital to my life.

If I'd been involved in multiple plane crashes I'd definitely not want to get back in a plane and I'd learn to live without flying no matter what. And, no, I don't even want to work at the airport either!

That was my decision made: for now I can live without policing.

23

Life after policing

When I finally came to the conclusion that I would leave, I had a mixture of emotions: sadness, regret, shame, relief, hope, but above all I just felt numb.

But as time moved on the negative emotions waned and the feeling of hope became stronger. I was still very poorly and I still struggled with huge anxiety, depression and complex PTSD but I was still here and still working on it.

I was not naive and I am definitely not stupid; I knew that I might never fully recover but I'd get up every day and try to be positive, hoping that one day I'd be able to say that I enjoyed living again and was not just enduring it.

What also became clear is that you really don't know how much pressure you're under until you're no longer under it.

I had a number of significant events: making the decision to leave; submitting an application for another job; being offered another job; submitting my formal resignation; and, finally, my last ever day as a police officer.

In truth, I had not been at work for many months, but I was still a police officer 24 hours a day, 365 days a year. I stopped carrying my warrant card as I was too unwell to deal with anything that may have happened while I was 'off-duty', and I felt it was a symbolic step if nothing else.

A close friend of mine who had left the police some months earlier helped me through this process and she said, 'The minute you press submit on your job application, you'll know.'

She was absolutely right. I pressed the button and it was as though time stood still but, despite that, the overwhelming feelings were of relief and hope. A new beginning.

I recently watched an incredibly inspiring video about wearing your scars proudly. It described how in Japan when pottery is broken, they repair the cracks with gold, silver or platinum. The art is called *kintsugi*. The Japanese believe it makes the object more beautiful as it shows that there is a history.

Kintsugi is often seen in a similar way to another Japanese philosophy called *wabi-sabi*. This is the embracing of something that is imperfect but in a positive way.

I felt pretty imperfect so it struck a chord with me.

It's the same for people: paint your struggles with gold and wear them as a badge of honour, as if to say, 'Look at what I've been through.' Wise words and something that definitely helped me as I am not ashamed, and I do wear my scars proudly. It also helped me deal with the stigma of mental health.

Someone asked me if I was really comfortable telling people what had happened and how badly affected I have been. It made me think: how can we truly deal with the stigma that is attached to mental ill health unless people are willing to talk openly?

I know that there may be people out there who I have encountered through my police work who will take great pleasure from knowing I've had such a tough time and have been so ill. That's life. That's a sad reality. I still feel that by telling my story, the benefit to others will far outweigh the negatives. And to those people who may take some pleasure, I hope that you never go through what I have, irrespective of who you are.

I watched the BBC documentary *A Royal Team Talk: Tackling Mental Health*, in which HRH Prince William and Dan Walker talked about some of the issues relating to mental health, particularly within football.

I thought it was incredibly positive and it will have done a huge amount of good, particularly by showing how some of the amazing players on the programme had suffered with mental health issues.

It also showed the true complexity of mental health. Prince William talked about wanting to show that people with poor mental health can still be in positions of leadership and power. I know exactly what he was saying: he wanted to reassure people that mental illness does not put you on the scrap heap and you can be successful. I completely agree but my illness left me lying in my bed, quietly crying and feeling like a complete failure.

I used to have a very responsible job, saving lives, tackling society's most dangerous criminals and leading a team of officers. There I was, now a shadow of my former self and unable to do any of that.

As the days went past I bounced back and recovered some of my confidence, but I think that it was important to say that success is different to everyone and, for some, just being here is a far greater achievement than owning their own business or having leadership positions. And they too deserve credit, support and admiration.

For me, getting up out of bed every morning, being able to go out in public and, more recently, being able to get a new job is success, and it is one of the greatest achievements of my life so far.

Having left the police I spent a number of months coming to terms with my illness and trying to work out what the future holds for me.

A key part of the work with Syd was looking at post-trauma growth. It sounds a strange concept and one that I initially failed to take on board. How can there be any 'growth' when I've lost the job I loved, I've suffered with agonising anxiety and my life has quite literally stalled?

But when you look, it's not all negative. I've become a much kinder, more compassionate person, someone who would move heaven and earth to help others. I've become more understanding, far more tolerant and far more forgiving. I've realised that you can't work every hour in the day and taking holidays is not a sign of weakness!

I've also set myself a challenge of telling my story to help raise awareness and ultimately help others. I've found that compassion is definitely a two-way street. I know that listening to other people who have suffered helped me hugely. By being compassionate and willing to talk openly about my mental health it will undoubtedly help other people. And I also benefit too. Being kind makes you feel good about yourself and that in turn makes life that little bit more positive.

This struggle has taught me a lot about myself. I worked a lot, far too much, in fact. I couldn't switch off and, ironically, when I was not at work I'd suffer with quite severe depressive symptoms – I guess this fuelled my unquenchable thirst for work.

I was completely addicted to policing. You may ask why. I have no idea, I just was. Maybe it was the buzz cops get when the big jobs go off, or perhaps it was being part of the team. I guess it was the whole package. I definitely had a sense of duty and wanted to make the community in which I grew up a better place, but beyond that I don't know.

I am, and always will be, someone who believes that if a job is worth doing it's worth doing properly.

I didn't look after my health – I'd eat badly, sleep badly and not take enough exercise, and I definitely drank far too much Diet Coke! I'd feel compelled to take on other people's problems and more importantly take responsibility for them, and I'd never say no.

I think some people took advantage of my willingness to help. I rarely had time for the people nearest and dearest to me, my friends and family. I missed far too many birthdays and Christmases. It wasn't all bad, though. I can now see I'm fundamentally a really honest, decent human being. I'd do anything for anyone if they needed help – friend or foe, I'd drop everything or get up in the middle of the night to help them. I'd even run into burning buildings if I thought someone needed help!

When you strip it all back you find out what your moral fibre really looks like. It has also taught me that your beliefs don't make you a better person, but your actions do, and that's what I'm going to focus on.

If there's one other thing this ordeal has taught me, it's this: be kind. And if you can't be kind, perhaps be quiet. That doesn't mean agreeing with everyone all the time or even liking everyone, but it does mean caring about others, irrespective of who they are.

The next time you criticise or insult someone, take a moment to try and see it from their point of view; you don't know their struggles. They are human too.

I've been on medication for months and the dosage has doubled and doubled and doubled again, and yet the best medicine I've had is compassion and kindness. If only I could keep doubling that.

Take a moment today to do something kind – speak to the person sat on their own, ask someone if they are OK, call that friend or relative who you've not spoken to for a while, send a nice email, thank someone, say hello to a stranger or check on your elderly neighbour.

If you see someone sat on a train silently crying, sit with them and, even if you don't know what to say, just be there for them. If you do something kind today, why not do something kind every day? It'll make the world a much better place.

And, above all, be kind to yourself. You deserve it.

Now that I am no longer a cop, I've been thinking about how that kindness would look in an organisation such as the police. It doesn't seem that difficult to me.

Be honest, open and genuine; care about how people feel; spend time checking on colleagues' welfare; if being critical, be professional and consider the impact – it's not what you say, it's the way you say it; people make mistakes, we all do, so be understanding; don't get involved in gossip; say thank you; be positive; remember that you've never walked in their shoes; don't allow disagreements to become personal or vindictive; offer support to colleagues and don't leave people behind; share the workload and be generous with your time and support; nothing is more important than looking after each other.

Crucially, this kindness and compassion must apply to everyone from the top to the bottom of an organisation.

Too many times I've seen senior officers suffer a character assassination at the hands of a canteen full of PCs, but they are also just doing their best and they suffer the same feelings of isolation as everyone else.

I recall one instance when a chief inspector had to post a member of staff to a different department. They will have wrestled with that decision, weighing up who would go and, importantly, why.

They then took the time to sit down with the officer and explain their reasoning; they showed that they cared and, to be blunt, they didn't have to, they're a chief inspector. A bit like in the film *Hot Fuzz*, a chief inspector can just make people disappear!

The treatment and criticism that boss got was wholly uncalled for and it made me realise just how perverse life can be sometimes. But the police is an amazing family to work for and I hope it stays that way for many years to come.

Now that I'm living through this I can tell you that mental ill health is debilitating, distressing, destructive and truly exhausting. It can consume you.

I had days when I was so overwhelmed with anxiety and a lack of hope that I couldn't really function. I'd spend every second of every minute, every minute of every hour, every hour of every day, every day of every week and every week of every month battling it. And for many, many months the struggle went on.

It is really hard to describe just how tough it can be, but I guess I'd liken it to a physical injury. Imagine how you'd feel if you'd been hit by a bus. You would have suffered lots of very serious physical injuries, which would completely incapacitate you and may even put your life in danger. Over time, hopefully with good care and treatment, the acuteness of those injuries would reduce but in all likelihood you'd be left with some residual problems that may flare up from time to time.

Some people will make a better recovery than others, but very few would come out of it totally unscathed and return to their previous level of wellbeing. That is how I feel with my mental health – the acute anxiety and depression have reduced but there is now a residual tension and mental dissonance, which on a good day is just there in the background and on a bad day still envelops me.

And I am not alone.

So that's what happened to me. Did I hit rock bottom? Yes. Am I embarrassed it happened to me? No. Should I be? I don't think so. Did I see it coming? Definitely not. Do I know what triggered it? Not specifically. Am I fully recovered? No. Do I think I will fully recover? I doubt it. Do I still feel anxious sometimes? Absolutely, every single day. Do I still sit at home and cry from time to time? Yes. Can I make life-at-risk decisions like I used to? Unfortunately not. Can I still talk the talk? You better believe it. Can I still walk the walk? Not at the moment. Do I feel scared about the future? A hundred per cent. Do I wish this hadn't happened to me? Yes, but nobody can turn back time. Am I broken beyond repair? Possibly. Do I still want to help others? Every day. Can I keep putting on the uniform? No. This is the end of my watch.

If you're reading this and you're going through a tough

time then I hope you find the strength to get through whatever is causing you so much distress at the moment. There are a lot of good people out there who will help you. I certainly know I will.

Be kind to yourself. You deserve it.

24

Good riddance

FINALLY, THE DAY that I had been dreading arrived. I knew that it would and I had been trying to prepare myself.

In truth, it was one of the hardest days I'd had since my breakdown all those months before. I had spent a long time thinking about sharing my story and I decided it was important. I am a great advocate that your beliefs don't make you a better person but your actions do. I believed strongly that mental health is a part of life but that people perhaps don't 'get' it and that it needs to be part of a much bigger conversation. I also believed that the police, along with some other professions, carry a huge risk when it comes to the mental health of their staff. So, if I believed that, I needed to do what I could to help raise awareness and break down that stigma.

I think it's fair to say that believing it was a good idea was quite easy; the action bit wasn't!

I also think that experience is almost completely useless unless you use it to benefit other people. Too often people go through their lives gaining valuable experiences but to little or no avail to others. I'd been in the fortunate position where I had experienced so much of life and the harsh realities of it, so to share my experiences to help others was a high priority as soon as I felt strong enough to do it.

I made contact with BBC Radio Suffolk as there were people there I'd worked with throughout my career and more recently on a weekly *Crime Beat* show.

I considered them friends and thoroughly decent people, so it made me feel confident in sharing my story through them. They were delighted to hear from me, as I had disappeared off the radar at the point that I became poorly, so it was great to get back in touch. Everyone was keen to know why 'Supercop' had left the police and this was the time for me to tell them.

We agreed a date and time; there was no going back now. The night before the interview I was petrified. I lay in bed with my mind racing at a million miles an hour. What would people say? What would people think? Would people be unkind? Would people believe me? Would I be able to get through the interview without breaking down?

It's fair to say I didn't sleep well at all and I certainly didn't feel rested when I got up the next morning. I arrived at the studios, which is a place very familiar to me and was somewhere that I usually felt incredibly welcome and at home. Not today! My heart was beating out of my chest, my legs were weak and my mouth was dry. I was anxious, really anxious.

I rang the buzzer and I was led to the green room that I knew so well.

After a few minutes the show's producer, Sally Burch, came out to see me. She knows that I don't do hugs, but she wrapped her arms around my slightly trembling body and said how nice it was to see me. That made me feel a whole lot better; a familiar, friendly face and someone I trusted greatly. She may not have realised just how important that was.

Then it was time to go into the studio. I took my usual seat opposite the presenter.

Mark Murphy is a charismatic and engaging man, skilfully holding three conversations at once while operating the banks of dials and microphones on the desk in front of him.

It sounds a curious thing to say, but radio studios are not the easiest place to have any conversation, as you have to constantly keep working out how long you've got before you're back on air.

Mark looked across and gave me a quick rundown on how the interview would go. He gave me a smile and said, 'You'll be fine, I'll look after you.'

I was now definitely feeling ready. Between them, Mark and Sally had put me at ease and it was time for me to share my story.

Mark introduced me: 'A former police sergeant with Suffolk Police is joining us this morning to talk exclusively about his career and how it came to an end. Dubbed Robocop for his arrest record, former Sergeant Ali Livingstone made five thousand arrests in fifteen years and became quite well known for it.'

It then cut to a series of headlines relating to my career, arrests and bravery awards being the main themes.

Mark started by asking me how things were when I started my career. I replied, 'When I first joined I didn't really know what I was getting into and I think, now that I look back on my career, that's quite common for people because it's really difficult to understand the complexities of policing until you're in it. Very soon after arriving it did feel that I'd hit the ground running. I really, really enjoyed the camaraderie and working with the team and I found that giving back was really rewarding.'

It was also interesting that my arrests had steadily declined as my work had gradually changed focus. 'My arrests became less and less and I took on lots of other roles; I was a tactical advisor to senior officers and I was a hostage and crisis negotiator, which for me was probably the most rewarding because it took me right back to the essence of why I joined the job, which was to help people in crisis . . .'

As the interview progressed, people started to contact the radio station. Mark read one out, 'Neil has been in touch on Twitter, "Ali is a good man, a guy who was 100 per cent committed to the police service."'

I knew Neil well as he was the sergeant who'd interviewed me as an eighteen-year-old when I became a special constable. It was nice to feel warmth and support during what was proving to be an emotionally draining interview.

When I had first got in touch with Mark and Sally I had told them that I really didn't like survivors who then claim to be experts so I wanted to make that really clear: 'I'm not an expert in mental health, I can only share what's happened to me.'

I certainly didn't think, however, that what I had to say was irrelevant.

Mark was really interested to know how my colleagues had reacted and particularly because it was me.

I explained, 'I had a text from a friend who now works in London and I haven't spoken to them for many years. They had spotted something on Twitter and thought "it looks like Ali's left the job". They texted me on Friday and they said, "I just cannot believe what you're telling me, I cannot believe you've left . . ."'

I had agreed with Mark that I did not want to talk about my new job. It was not relevant, and I wanted some time out of the spotlight.

It seemed an appropriate moment to talk about success, though, particularly in relation to recovery.

'It's interesting because I watched a documentary . . . there was a conversation about if you've got mental health you can still be a CEO, you can still lead a company. I remember thinking you can, but I can't, not right now. But I can work, I can get a job and get up every day . . . and for me that's real success. What I would say to anyone listening with mental health, your measure of success is totally down to you. If you're still here and still getting by and still working, then all credit to you. So yeah, on to the next chapter.'

A listener contacted the station and Mark read out her message: 'Fascinating interview this morning about the decision to retire due to mental health, such an incredibly honest and engaging account.'

Then another message, this time from a former colleague: 'Ali always cared about his colleagues around him and I wish him every success and happiness for the future.'

That meant a great deal to me because I did care a huge amount about the people I worked with.

'If there is one legacy, and I know my arrests will be one of them, I hope that people who worked with me, and also some of the people who I dealt with, think, "Do you know what, he was a fair, kind, compassionate guy doing the job that he did and he did it well." '

I also hope that sooner or later, mental health will be a 'non-issue' that is just part of life.

The response I got after the interview was truly humbling and it summed up why I was baring my soul to the world: I wanted to help people. This was not for my benefit, this was not for some egotistical gain, it was to show people that it is OK not to be OK.

As I walked out of the studio, I felt a huge sense of pride and achievement. I had put it out there and there was now no going back.

Before I knew it, I was on my way to speak to the local TV station. Again, it was someone who I knew well, one of life's genuine nice guys, always pleased to see you and more often than not having a laugh and a joke. I met him and the cameraman in Christchurch Park.

It was a beautiful morning and there was a gentle buzz of activity with people enjoying the summer sunshine and quietly going about their daily business. I spent an hour or two talking about what had happened and, despite the tranquil setting and good company, I can't say that I ever felt totally comfortable.

Had it not been for the greater good that I hoped it would do, I'd have happily walked away. But this was important so it had to be done.

I have been asked many times if I was sure that I was happy to share my experience. I thought long and hard about that, particularly as I had no doubt there would be people I had dealt with over the years who would take great delight in seeing their old adversary now suffering.

I was happy to share my experience as the good far outweighed the bad. It came sharply into focus, though, when I was asked if I was happy for an article to appear online. I knew it would be searchable in the future and it could, for example, be seen by future employers. That was the issue of the mental health stigma encapsulated and crystallised in one brief conversation. Why would me being poorly in 2018 have any relevance on my employability in years to come? And if an employer did feel that, then I'd certainly not want to be working for them anyway! Interesting nonetheless.

That incident made up my mind, though. I was not speaking to anyone else; not because I didn't want to share my story any more but because just that one comment had knocked me for six and I had to balance my wellbeing with raising awareness.

In any case, I'd said what I felt I needed to. I walked back home with my mind absolutely racing. I'd been warned before about committing career suicide when I told the Chief Constable that I didn't want his staff officer job; perhaps I'd really done it now.

I began running over and over again exactly what I had said and how a future employer might react if they listened to that interview or read that article.

As had become common with me, my thoughts began careering away from me, and before I knew it, hours had passed and I'd ended up at the inevitable catastrophic conclusion that my life was in a mess, I'd lose my new job and never work again.

Fortunately, over the next few hours the positive responses I received from far and wide completely eclipsed any concerns and my new, stronger mindset gradually made sense of those irrational thoughts.

I finished the day by reading an article that had been written in the local paper about me. I felt it was a really good piece of journalism and it covered a great deal of my career and also the struggles I had endured.

I then apprehensively worked my way down to the comments section. 'Good riddance to this extreme nut-job.' I've unfortunately encountered this type of behaviour throughout my service, but take a moment to think about it. A deliberate comment, at the bottom of an article which laid out for all to see the mental ill health I'd suffered.

I was in a place where it caused me no distress but it shocked me that someone would think this was acceptable. If they hoped to offend me or upset me, they failed miserably as it simply motivated me even more.

As the day drew to a close, I also had a chance to reflect on what had been written and broadcast. My story was appearing in newspapers and websites far beyond Ipswich. I was emotionally and mentally drained. It had perhaps taken more out of me than I'd anticipated.

I am by my very nature a private person; perhaps that has come from years of policing, meaning that I'm guarded about my personal life. There is no doubt my police career had been high profile and Sergeant Ali Livingstone had never been far from the news, but this was different. This was Ali Livingstone, the ex-police officer who was now sharing his mental health issues and treatment. Something that is so personal and so sensitive, but it was now headline news.

Over the next week I was inundated with enquiries from national media outlets for interviews. I politely declined them all. Without fail, every refusal was met with a level of understanding and supportive personal acknowledgement; maybe we are starting to understand mental health after all!

Some journalists shared personal experiences of mental health and others just offered their support and encouragement. I am truly thankful to them for being so compassionate with me and it certainly made me realise that there are good people in all professions.

Having gone to the media, my mental health was now out there. All of a sudden my friends and acquaintances from outside the police knew what had been going on for the previous eighteen months.

As I expected, they were unbelievably supportive but some were almost a little cross. Why had I not felt able to tell them? What sort of person did I think they were? They wished that they had known so that they could have helped along the way.

An awful lot of them apologised, suddenly realising that they'd spent the previous year or more asking me about my work, unaware that I was off and that the mere mention of policing would fill me with terror. I felt bad that I had not been honest with them, and if I had my time again I'd have been upfront from the beginning.

What it did show me, though, was just how invisible mental health can be. I had been so poorly, so low, so traumatised and yet the vast majority of people around me knew nothing about it. I had put on a brave face for so long and almost lived two parallel lives.

Some people may think that means that a mental health issue is not a serious illness; that's not my experience at all; it's just something that for some reason I felt I had to hide at all costs.

I had been exposed to the physical effects of mental illness; the unavoidable and uncontrollable physiological symptoms that made me feel as poorly as I had ever been. It also put huge logistical pressures on me; it would sometimes take me hours to build myself up to going into work or attending a meeting, and some nights I'd barely sleep at all.

In truth, I was disabled and yet the majority of people had no idea because they couldn't see it and I wasn't telling them.

During this time, I was still receiving treatment from the mental health services. My time with Syd had been so incredibly positive but I was now being looked after by a team of specialists who were going to try and unpick the issues and put me back together again.

The doctor who I was seeing was a lovely lady, very softly spoken, calm and reassuring. She had an incredibly warm manner and a smile that would immediately put you at ease.

Over the weeks we talked about my inability to choose a path and stick with it. 'I just feel like I can't settle, it's like my life is in constant turmoil.'

I think that she sensed my genuine frustration and angst. I'd found being in this constant state of flux to be truly exhausting.

She paused, sat back and then softly said, 'Ali, I think that you're just a sampler.'

'A sampler?' I'd never heard that before.

She continued, 'When you find something you like then you'll know it's right.' Instantaneously I quite liked being a sampler. It was such a positive way of describing something that had been so troubling to me and, I imagine, lots of people around me.

She carried on, 'It's a bit like trying different foods: you can keep trying different dishes until you find the ones that you really like.'

It seemed like such a trivial, almost silly way to describe it, but it was absolutely right. That's what life is, one big adventure where you try different things and learn what you like and, importantly, what you don't. No longer was I indecisive or confused, I was just trying things out; a bit like test-driving cars!

I spent a lot of time thinking about what the future may hold for me. I, like many other people, always had targets and goals. I was seldom happy with where I was at any one time so I was always thinking, *What next?*

The first job didn't quite work out as expected. It was never going to be easy starting any job having been in the police for so many years, and this one didn't seem to suit me as much as I had hoped. Maybe it was just too soon. I decided that I'd apply for a few different roles and see how I got on. I was still definitely sampling! I then had the awful realisation that I'd have to hope that my mental health issues and the recent media coverage didn't mean I remained on the scrapheap.

I remember applying for one job and it asked for an example of some personal or professional development that I had done; a typical question on an application form that gets prospective employees wracking their brains. As part of my treatment we had talked about what I had gone through as post-trauma growth, but never had I thought I'd use it as an example of personal development on a job application! This was my opportunity. I had suffered with debilitating PTSD, depression and anxiety, and I had come through the worst of it a far better, wiser, happier person. I now had a much greater understanding of something that is everywhere in life and, just as importantly, I had come to realise just how important it was to be compassionate.

I sent off my application and I guess they agreed as I got an interview. I'd learnt a whole new set of skills and had experience of something that at some time, to a greater or lesser extent, will touch everyone's lives.

But, having got the job, and having had such a positive and supportive experience with the media when I first told my story, I felt very let down when I arrived at my new role.

Prior to starting, a journalist had been in touch with my new boss to find out what my role would be and wanting more information. The same journalist was aware that I did not want that as I had been telling my story about my policing career and mental health struggles, but I'd made it clear I wanted to start a new career without the media spotlight on me. The journalist even had my contact details so they could have easily called me and spoken to me, but no, they decided to contact my new boss out of the blue.

That made me feel ill; sick to the stomach. My first few days were far more traumatic as a result and showed a lack of understanding of mental health.

In the time after leaving the police I also had the opportunity to really think back to how I had been when I was poorly. Something that I spent time contemplating was just how consumed I had been with suicidal thoughts. I must be clear, I never had any intention to hurt myself and yet it was at the forefront of my mind all day, every day.

I thought back to how I had talked to so many 'suicidal' people over the years as a hostage and crisis negotiator, and how as a society we almost seem scared to call mental ill health what it is. I'd lost count of how many times I'd heard people refer to 'dark' or 'troubling' thoughts. It was almost as though to be unequivocal and clear was too much to bear.

Can you imagine having chest pains and not being able to just say it, instead referring to 'troubling pains' or 'worrying sensations'? The doctors would think you'd gone mad. No, you've got chest pains!

I hope that as time moves on and people become more understanding, no longer will people feel ashamed or worried about being honest. I'd hate to think that people are suffering as I was and feel unable to tell someone exactly how they were feeling.

Leaving the police was always going to be a massive challenge. It's such a unique job and you spend an awful lot of time with your colleagues. There will be colleagues who I have shared more Christmas Days with than my own family. Cops often socialise together and will spend hours talking about 'the job'. That has all gone now I am no longer in the club.

In the early days I was still in daily contact with former colleagues and in some ways that made me feel better; less isolated, I guess. But that's not moving on and that was not what I needed for my mental health. My anxiety and trauma were centred on policing, so leaving was a fundamental part of getting healthy again.

I suddenly realised just how often I was being contacted by cops. How many WhatsApp groups I was in for various social nights out. I was no longer a police officer but I was still in contact with people from that life just as much. That all had to stop. I had to reduce that down and that was tough. It was time to go cold turkey! These were people who had stood by me through thick and thin, friends who had been there when I really needed them, people I trusted with my life. We all needed to go through a readjustment and that would take time.

I stopped meeting people as much and threw myself into making new friends away from policing. It really was time to move on. I'd often think about how similar my position would be to those professional footballers who come to the end of their playing days and find themselves stepping out into the real world. I can imagine that football was their life, in the same way that policing was mine, and now they had to try and find a new path.

The sense of isolation was immense and at times, and when I had time to stop and think, I'd feel overwhelmed. Those same people will always be my friends, and I will spend time with them, but I'll never be able to be as immersed in those friendships as I once was.

Over the next few months, though, I settled into life and things were good again. I lost count of the number of people who commented on me being like a different person. I'd spent so many years under such extreme pressure that it was inevitable that it had affected every aspect of my life. And it's true, you don't know how much pressure you're under until you're not under it any more. I was now so much more relaxed and I was thankful to be happy and content.

I also had the chance to spend some time enjoying things that I'd never really had the time to do. I'd often thought that my work defined who I was as a person, and subsequently my mental health would define me yet further. I think I was wrong on both counts.

Until I left the police I would not have been able to imagine my life not being Sergeant Livingstone, but life goes on and I am my own person. I can't change the fact that my job undoubtedly changed me, mainly for the good I hasten to add. It exposed me to things that have had a profound effect on my outlook and perspective on life – I find it hard to get too worked up about things because in the grand scheme of things they are pretty inconsequential. I sometimes see people being swept away in the moment and it brings a wry smile to my face as it means that they can't have too much to worry about in life.

The job has also left me with an overwhelming desire to try and make things better. It sounds clichéd but it is completely sincere. I spent so many years dealing with the aftermath of traumatic events that I have been left determined to do what I can to stop anyone reaching that point.

As I stepped on to this new path, I was so much more comfortable with who I was and what had happened to me. I didn't regret it. I didn't feel ashamed. I did sometimes feel anxious and overwhelmed, but who doesn't?

My resilience was getting stronger and stronger every day and no longer would I wake up at night, trembling uncontrollably or gripped with anxiety. I started a job where I felt I could genuinely help people again, just like policing, but perhaps without the trauma and pressures.

I think it's fair to say that I had crammed more policing into my eighteen years than some would see in twice that time, and it was now time to use that experience and knowledge to help young people.

Am I fixed? No. I still sometimes feel very alone in this world and my mental health will be something that I have to closely monitor.

On several occasions I've almost allowed myself to slip back into that unrelenting, almost obsessive work ethic, but through the treatment I've had, I've spotted it. I've realised how much I miss policing and, as time has gone on, I've realised how much experience I gained.

Now that I am in a much healthier place, who knows what the future holds?

25

Lessons learnt

I GUESS THAT YOU can't go through a career as varied and intense as mine without coming out the other side with a few ideas on what the police do and what the challenges are that lie ahead. I've certainly learnt that the police is a forever-changing machine that sometimes changes so quickly you don't know if you're coming or going.

New legislation, new policies, new powers, new recruitment requirements; it seems that there is barely a day that goes by without yet another change being announced. I sometimes wished that the change could just slow down, not because I was averse to it but because the police struggle to land anything properly before moving on to the next big issue.

I've come to accept that the police can't do everything and that the public just need to be aware of that. There is a finite number of cops and police staff, and the demand often far outweighs the resources the police have to deal with it.

I'd often chat to older people and they would bemoan the fact that they now don't see a police officer walking the beat and they blame the government and the police themselves. Unfortunately, some of the demands are often out of sight and therefore out of mind for the public: counterterrorism, safeguarding vulnerable people, cybercrime and historic sexual offences to name a few. I can assure you, cops would love to be out and about all day long, but that just isn't possible.

I've certainly come to accept that policing is a game of chasing the risk wherever it may be. That does mean that sometimes things get missed or ignored completely but that's a reality and until the police numbers are rebuilt that is the new status quo.

The austerity measures over the last few years have really hurt the police along with all the public services. It is laughable that government and a few senior leaders within the police felt that they couldn't just state the bleeding obvious – fewer cops will result in higher crime! If we can't accept that simple correlation then either the public are being intentionally misled or the people in positions of power are inexcusably out of touch and lacking in basic common sense.

I do feel that austerity across the public sector also disproportionately affected the work of the police because it is often the emergency service of last resort. What I mean by that is that when other organisations fail to meet their obligations, it will be the police who have to step in and fill the void, often to prevent harm.

An example that I would see day after day over many years was how mental health services have leaned more and more on the police to assist them with their work. I certainly don't blame the practitioners as they are at the coalface trying to keep up with an overwhelming demand and doing an amazing job in an unenviable position, but the situation cannot go on indefinitely.

Keeping the public safe is not just a responsibility of the police; health, education, social services and local authorities all have a part to play but all of them are feeling the strain as well.

I've come to realise that the people the police deal with are a tiny minority in society. The overwhelming majority of the public have little or no contact with the police and, from my perspective, that is what they want. They are reassured knowing the police are out there, doing whatever the police do, but they hope that they never have to call upon their services.

It does show just how dysfunctional society is, though, that it's a tiny number of people who commit a huge proportion of offences and impact so heavily on their communities. I was once asked to collate a list of top offenders to be targeted as part of a proactive operation aimed at driving down crime. I was told that the list must not have more than one hundred offenders on it. Despite having made almost five thousand arrests, the list only got to about fifty and then I was really scraping the barrel for truly prolific offenders. If those people were stopped from committing offences the crime rate in Suffolk would literally plummet overnight. And the same would be true of so many other places.

It really is important that policing can focus on those that cause the most harm.

If I could change one thing in the police it would be that cops need to be kinder to each other in general. When the chips are down and the pressure is on the police are really good at what they do but it's so easy to forget that they're all just people with their own issues too.

Police officers need to stick together and look after each other – and not just when things go wrong.

What also came out of the early weeks after my breakdown was that there seemed to be a lack of compassion out there in the big bad world too. We don't even show compassion to ourselves sometimes so how can we expect to see it from others?

Just think about it: you read the news every day and people are being vilified and criticised without a moment's consideration of the effect that could have, and we've all been guilty of jumping on the bandwagon. There's a person behind that story and on the scantest of details we've condemned them and cast them aside, oblivious or, even worse, not caring what damage that will do.

I recall an interview in which a journalist said that the apparent mental breakdown and suicidal thoughts of the person he was interviewing were 'very convenient'. Knowing what I've been through, that took my breath away. It reminded me of my train journey to London and the isolation I felt.

I guess as a police officer it felt like we got it worse than others – the cops can't do right for doing wrong sometimes and the standards by which the police are judged are biased and unfair.

I sometimes see the support that the public give the other emergency services, the NHS and the military, and just wish the police could get that same overt display of warmth and support. Good cops are being damaged, some beyond repair, and yet they are only doing their best. At times of feeling overwhelmed and vulnerable, that support would make all the difference.

I walk away having served almost two decades with the most professional police service in the world. It is full of ordinary people doing an extraordinary job to the very best of their ability, but they are becoming battle weary and tired.

The British model of policing is unique and is something that we must maintain at all costs; the police rely on the public just as much as the public rely on the police, and never has it been more important to maintain and grow that relationship than now. The police must never forget that they police by consent and, as such, ask what would the public expect from them. The public also have their part to play: remember that the cops that you are dealing with are also members of the public and they need *your* help too.

There are big challenges ahead and the police need all the support they can get.

I leave the police with my head held high having made some amazing friends and put in a real shift. I am very proud of what I achieved as a police officer and the contribution that I have made. When I look back on my career, I loved it, just about every minute of it. I have not left the police because I didn't like the job any more, I left because for now my playing days are over. Emotionally and mentally I can't do it all over again and it is time for a change.

I genuinely wish all the cops out there all the best and I just want to say to them: keep fighting the good fight. It's the toughest of jobs but the overwhelming majority of the public have your back and support you. I certainly know that I do. And remember, you're never just a number. Take care.

26

Going back

When I left the police I never, ever envisaged that I'd return to law enforcement. I felt that it would always be something that I used to do, something that I did once upon a time and gradually it would disappear further and further into the distance as I looked in the rear-view mirror of my life.

As I left the organisation, the Chief Constable, Steve Jupp, took me out for a coffee and he said to me, 'Stay in touch, Ali, and remember the door is always open.'

I walked out of the coffee shop thinking, 'That's really nice of him, but I'm never coming back. Never in a million years!'

Having left the police I went to work in education and it was one of the best things I have ever done. I became a pastoral officer at a high school, looking after a year group of over 250 eleven-year-olds!

In some ways I felt completely ill qualified, but having supervised a team of highly excitable and at times immature police officers it actually stood me in very good stead indeed. It was also a job that revolved around people and I'd spent my whole working life specialising in that.

People would sometimes ask, 'What do you actually do then?' Good question. My role was to help with anything that got in the way of a child's learning; behaviour, attendance, problems at home, bullying, mental health, the list goes on and on and on. Pastoral officers are 'fixers' who try and keep things on track and moving in the right direction.

Lots of older people would often comment, 'We never had that in my day,' and they are right. What I would say, though, is that I think that life is more complicated now. I certainly know that I wouldn't want to swap places with a child today. I liked things the way they were when I grew up. They seemed a lot simpler back then.

High schools are busy, hectic and at times incredibly tough places to work. Before I started I remember thinking how easy life must be for teachers – they only work for part of the year, they have lots of holidays, there are no shifts and certainly no working weekends.

Little did I know just how intense education would be. I walked into the school on my first day and it was like a different world to the one that I had been living in for the previous two decades.

Schools just feel slightly removed from reality, which is ironic because they are such a fundamental part of everyone's upbringing. There is a hustle and bustle, a sense of things happening; the day would ebb and flow. The school campus starts very quietly and then as the staff and children begin arriving the energy levels increase and you're off and running.

I think that what working in a school showed me, above all, is that life is good, life should be fun and the more people can smile and laugh, the better it is for everyone.

If children can do one thing better than adults, it's having fun! I spent a lot of time laughing and smiling the days away.

I remember one day in particular when I arrived outside my office to find six of my Year 7 boys covered from head to toe in mud. Shoes, trousers, coats, hands, faces and hair. Covered! That was pretty impressive as it wasn't even 9 a.m. and the school day hadn't started yet.

It transpired that a little high jinks and play fighting had got out of hand and it all then went a bit medieval with them slipping and sliding all over the place and ending up in a very muddy heap. Fortunately, nobody got hurt and they all accepted their part in it. No harm done and just a lot of very muddy uniforms to wash.

Having worked at the school for three or four months, my health was now in a much better place. My map of the world was changing; no longer was it littered with people doing bad things to each other. In the main children are unwaveringly kind and honest.

I remember one occasion where I was told about a little lad who had no pens or pencils. His family were not able to afford much and he was therefore having to borrow things from his classmates. I went straight out and bought him a pencil case, complete with everything that he needed – pens, pencils, rulers and rubbers. I gave it to him later that day and his smile said it all.

A few hours later I heard a gentle knock on the office door; it was the little lad.

'Sir, I've brought you a cookie from the canteen to say thank you.'

I guess that my smile said it all too. It's not hard to see why schools can be such uplifting places to work.

The staff were also incredible. Teachers are amazingly passionate about their work; they just care and want to do the best by the children. I also had the pleasure to work with a lot of our teaching assistants and staff who worked within learning support. I was in awe of their drive, determination and patience in helping children who had all sorts of difficulties to overcome.

The staff were fully committed to the pupils and there were no half measures.

There was one team in particular, the THRIVE team, with whom I spent many hours. In my school they worked with a very small cohort of children who needed specialist help during their first couple of years at high school to help them along the way.

I remember walking into their classroom for the first time – it was a small room but it was littered with colourful posters, rewards charts, toys and pieces of work. It had a warm, safe and welcoming feel about it but that had nothing to do with the room or any of the objects or materials in it; it had everything to do with the staff. They would feel the highs and the lows that their pupils were experiencing, sometimes feeling desperately helpless but at other times feeling true elation.

My policing career often involved us helping people and sometimes seeing them at their lowest point, but no sooner had we arrived, we'd be leaving. I'd never worked in an environment where you see the people you are helping every single day. At times, it was incredibly tough and you just wanted to make things better.

I remember going to one of the THRIVE staff meetings after school and they told me that they had a present for me. It was one of their rainbow-coloured lanyards. The only people in the school who had them were the THRIVE team so I was absolutely made up to become an honorary member; it made me feel quite emotional!

Their supervisor is a truly inspirational man, loved by the children and held in the highest regard by the staff. We're lucky to have people like him and his team around to help our youngsters flourish.

Working in a school wasn't all sunshine and light, though. It could be incredibly stressful and pretty confrontational at times.

I recall one parent who came to see me; he was absolutely furious about something that had happened. He called me early one morning, 'Stop talking and listen to me. I'm on my way up there and you better be ready!'

It sounded pretty unpleasant and it reminded me of the aggression and hostility that is aimed at police officers. Maybe he was hoping to intimidate me. If he was then he would have been disappointed. In some ways it felt so different to policing, but in others it was just the same – the angry tone, the gritted teeth and the aggressive posturing.

As the meeting got under way there was lots of hot air and grandstanding, but when push came to shove, he calmed down before he was shown the door. As it happened, the meeting was a very positive one and we parted ways with a handshake.

While working at the school I also went back to give some presentations to the police. It was the first time that I had spoken so openly about what had happened. It was part of a series of wellbeing days so it seemed a perfect chance to tell my story and hopefully prevent others going the same way that I did.

I started the presentation with a slide showing a photo of me in my uniform just about to go out on patrol. It was a really nice picture and importantly it was two days before my breakdown. It showed how unexpected it had been.

The presentations went really well and I was blown away by the responses I had. I covered my work before my breakdown and the pressures that I felt. I also spent a long time talking about my treatment and recovery. I already knew that a lot of former colleagues were particularly interested to hear my story because it was me and so it proved!

The presentations also helped me a great deal too; each time I went in to present, it felt easier and easier. HQ was like my home and it made me realise just how comfortable I am there. In some ways it was like a time warp when I'd go in and see so many familiar and friendly faces.

As time went on, I became increasingly aware of how well I was feeling. My anxiety was no longer a part of my everyday life; in fact, it was something that I barely thought about. At one point, it had consumed me every single waking moment; not any more. My sleep was restful and plentiful and I no longer worried about going to certain places or meeting certain people.

Something that had always stuck in my mind was when I suddenly realised that, when I was driving in my car, I'd be singing along to the music. It seems such a daft thing but, for so many months, I hadn't. I was now playing my sport again, enjoying socialising and life just felt back under control.

I had returned to normality, but a far healthier one than before. I had got a perspective back that, in truth, I had probably been missing for many years.

As my anxiety diminished, it left me with a sense of what I had lost and the job that I had walked away from. It made me feel quite low, but this time it was different, as I wasn't depressed.

I could do something about it. I loved being someone who would step forward when others were stepping back. I loved tackling injustice. I loved being part of a unique organisation. And I loved policing. It made me think, could I do it again? I thought long and hard about whether I'd want to do operational, front-line policing? Not now, not yet. I'd spent eighteen years wearing body armour and tackling some of the most dangerous people. Importantly, though, it was a well thought out, rational decision. What did I want to do? What would make me happy? And what would keep me healthy? The part that I really missed was the organisation and the sense of purpose that policing has, and that didn't mean being a police officer.

I was very conscious that I didn't want to do anything that could make me poorly again. I got the sense that some people didn't believe me when I'd say that. They remember the old Ali who was so driven that he just couldn't say no. I most definitely hit rock bottom in March 2018 and there was no way that I wanted to do anything that could send me back there.

As we entered a new decade it was time to take the plunge and apply for a role within policing. It came as a big surprise just how many police staff roles there are and how regularly they come up. I spent a few months looking and then I finally found one that I felt I would enjoy and one I'd be well qualified for.

I went to the interview and it felt very strange; I was someone that they knew so well but I was no longer part of their gang. I arrived for the interview and the lady on reception asked me what organisation I was with? I said, 'None, it's just me.'

The interview went well and I was offered the job as a member of police staff. I wouldn't be an officer but I would be able to use my years of experience to help officers investigating drugs cases.

Something that being poorly has done is give me a whole new nervousness about recruitment procedures. Generally speaking, if you're offered a job, that's it, it's in the bag! Lots of people will have completed medical questionnaires when they apply for jobs and not thought anything of it. Now that I've been through this period of mental ill health, it makes them all the more significant. It almost feels as though the recruitment process is split into two parts – the element that relates to whether you are professionally suitable for the job and then the element where they decide if you're fit for the role. Would they have me back? Would they think it's too soon? Would they decide that I'm just too high risk?

I decided to go and see Syd, the consultant psychologist who I worked with when I first had my breakdown. I sat in the same waiting room that I had visited on 26 March 2018, almost exactly two years earlier.

This time I wasn't trembling or anxiously staring at the floor. I was really looking forward to seeing someone who I considered to be a friend as well as a doctor. I also knew that he would be brutally honest with me: he'd tell me what he thought, not necessarily what I wanted to hear.

Syd works in a very old building situated on a quiet back road on the outskirts of the town centre. Other than the door code, everything else was just as I had remembered.

Having let myself in I walked down the narrow corridor and sat myself down in the small waiting room at the back of the building. After a few minutes I heard the floorboards begin to creak in the hallway and in walked Syd. 'Ali, come on in. It's great to see you.'

He had a beaming smile despite it being 8 a.m. on a Monday morning.

We chatted for an hour about what had been happening since I'd decided the leave the police some twelve months earlier. It was lovely to see him and explain just how much progress I'd made. He then asked, 'So why do you want to go back?'

That was the question I'd have to get used to answering. I explained how I'd been feeling and how well I felt that I'd recovered. 'I feel like my outlook on life has completely changed, I'm happy and I'm no longer impatient.'

I remember Syd telling me when I first met him, 'You need to be turned down, not turned off.' He was right. I will always be someone who needs a bit of pressure and a high workload to function healthily but most importantly now I knew how to manage that far better.

I have also come to realise that policing is a huge part of my life – it makes me tick, it makes me feel fulfilled and it makes me happy.

Syd had always been very reassuring, often telling me that eventually my 'threat' system would calm down and return to normal.

In truth I'm not sure if I ever completely believed him but I was prepared to wait and see. They say, 'Take away a man's hope and you take away his will to live.' I was happy to be hopeful.

Interestingly my threat system has probably returned to a far more normal state. At the height of my breakdown, it was on overdrive and made me feel on edge all day every day. For the years prior to my breakdown, however, I was desensitised to risk and violence and death. It just bounced off. I think that I now react in a far more 'normal' way – things that should scare me, do; things that are not that important, aren't; things that should be enjoyable, are; things that should make me laugh, do!

That's definitely some post-trauma growth, as it means my life will be far more enjoyable moving forward.

I left the school at the strangest of times, just as it closed due to the outbreak of coronavirus. Never before had the school closed under these circumstances and on the last day before we shut down it was the saddest of things to see.

The initial excitement that the children felt at the prospect of an extended 'holiday' soon evaporated and the realisation set in: this was serious.

As I said to my Year 7s, who had gathered around me in the playground, 'This is a moment in time and time stands still for nobody, not even Mr Livingstone!'

The last day made me realise just how far my mental health had come. I felt calm, composed and in control. There was no hint of catastrophising, something that had dominated my mindset for many months when I was ill. While others around me were feeling anxious and a little overwhelmed, I wasn't.

When I was poorly I set dates in the future and imagined what I'd be doing then – in six months, in a year, in five years. Any crisis has a habit of making you feel like you're frozen in time, like the clock has stopped. I suspect some people were feeling like that, particularly as significant events were being cancelled or postponed – exams, holidays, sporting events and even family gatherings. I immediately changed my focus to the future because time never stops.

We didn't know then when the lockdown would end but we knew it would. The school would reopen and the children return. We told each other, 'It may be in the spring, if not it will be in the summer, if not then in the autumn,' but we knew it would happen.

This return to policing is much more than just another job or another career. It's far more symbolic than that and far more significant. It shows that things can and do get better. It shows that despite how desperate you may be feeling, you just never know where your recovery will take you. It shows that time is a great healer.

I have experienced the highs and exhilaration of being a police officer and I then lived through the desolation and desperation of mental ill health. But I always had hope that things could and would get better.

I'd often say to people that I believed this was just a passage of time and I had to keep persevering.

And I still reflect on what was said during the BBC documentary about people being successful despite suffering with mental health problems. For me, re-joining is success, but for some success, will be coping with day-to-day life; being content; being healthy; being alive. I hope that as a society we learn to treat everyone as individuals and, no matter what, be kind.

While I was very poorly, I'd often listen to a particular song that gave me inspiration to keep going. It seemed to encapsulate my struggle but made me believe that I could get better.

Sometimes I'd listen to it for hours and hours, silently taking in the words. I'd only ever considered it linked to Liverpool Football Club, but listening to the words, it resonated with me and changed my perspective on life. At a time when I needed it most, it gave me hope.

'You'll Never Walk Alone' was written in the 1940s for Broadway by Rodgers and Hammerstein but made famous by

Merseybeat group Gerry and the Pacemakers in the 1960s, when it came to be associated with Liverpool FC.

I now have a framed picture of the lyrics on my wall at home and I read them often, particularly when things are hard.

It felt as though my mental breakdown was like walking through a storm, and I desperately tried to hold my head up high. I believe that's why I am not ashamed of what has happened to me.

I think that most people who have gone through anxiety and depression will feel like it's a dark and scary and lonely place. But, as the lyrics say and my story shows, at the end of the storm there can be a 'golden sky and the sweet silver song of a lark'.

I'd often silently tell myself to walk on and, despite how difficult it was, I always hoped that things would get better for me. I firmly believe that things can and will improve but you must keep moving forward, inch by inch – that's my experience and that is what I believe.

And, importantly, you're never on your own: there are people out there who will always help you.

As I head back into policing, I don't know what the future holds, but what I do know is that whatever life throws at me, I'm now ready again.

Acknowledgements

I'D LIKE TO thank Little, Brown for helping me to tell my story. I never imagined being a published author – I was always just a cop! From the moment I met Duncan Proudfoot, I liked him – a genuine, honest and kind gentleman, and someone I trusted and wanted to work with.

I was also helped hugely by Ben Ando, a thoroughly decent chap, who edited my manuscript with great skill and attentiveness – his knowledge and insight were invaluable and he has made it into what it is today.

Thanks to my friend Kate Arkell. She spent hours and hours reading drafts and giving her advice, long before it was sent to the publishers. I have no doubt that she helped make my dream come true of publishing a book!

Duncan, Ben and Kate, thank you.

I'd like to thank my family for their unwavering and unconditional support. They have been with me every step of the way during my career and have felt the highs and lows as much as I have. I have undoubtedly caused them some worrying moments along the way but I also hope that I have made them proud.

I have worked with some incredible people, the kind of people who you can trust and depend on, the kind of people you need in a crisis. I already knew that but having been so poorly brought it even more into focus.

I'd like to thank Richard Prouse for being there in my darkest hour and supporting me back to health. We met on our first day in the police and have become best friends since. I am lucky to have such a trusted confidant.

Thanks to Ben Cook for being the best boss I've ever worked for and someone who I can turn to whenever I need him. I loved working with Ben and they were some of the best days of my life. He is funny, kind, caring and loyal, and he went from being my best boss to being one of my best friends. A truly inspirational man.

I'd like to thank Stuart Weaver for being the best welfare officer I could ever have wished for. We had been friends and colleagues for many years but his care and support when I was ill was incredible. His kindness and compassion were outstanding and I will never be able to articulate just how grateful I am.

Thanks to Dr Syd Hiskey, my consultant psychologist. His knowledge and professionalism were never in doubt but, importantly, his kindness and compassion were equal in measure. At a time when I had no hope and nowhere to turn, he helped me. I cannot thank him enough and consider him to be a friend as well as my doctor.

Thanks also to the friends and colleagues who were there for me when I needed them most – Kev Lee, Matt Bodmer, Ali Maidment, Tim Barrell, Nick Shirley, Rocky Hussain, John Ford, Barry Harman, Nicola Turner, Claire Yates, Steve Clark, Andy Kirk, Steve Mattin, Tonya Antonis, Jen Eves and Ian Rafferty. They've been constant features in such a large part of my life over many years. I shall never forget your continued support and kindness.

I'd like to thank everyone who played their part on NRT3 over the years. It wasn't just a response team; it was a family and they were some of the best days of my life.

Away from policing, I am so lucky to have friends who are equally caring and kind. I'd like to thank each and every one of them – in particular, I'd like to thank Gill and Mike Muncaster, Denis Groualle, Darius and Gill Fylan, Adrian Howell, Emily Ison, Kristian Day and Ryan Betts. You are such important people to me and I feel very blessed to be able to call each of you my friend.

I'd also like to thank Mike Penman, my squash coach from the age of nine years old. I was awestruck from the day I met him and he played a colossal role not only in my sport, but also in my formative years. He taught me how to be kind, how to be brave, how to be tough, how to be honest and how to be humble. He also taught me how to have fun! He has been a huge influence and I owe him an awful lot.

Finally I'd like to thank and acknowledge my dear late friend, Peter Robinson. He was a huge supporter of mine going through school and then when I joined the police. He was a larger than life, charismatic man and someone who could always make me laugh and smile. We'd spend hours talking and I'd listen intently to him imparting his wisdom and knowledge. I still miss him greatly and know that he'd have loved to read my book.

There are so, so many others that I'd love to thank, in particular the incredible colleagues that I've worked with over the years and the amazing friends that I have. They all know who they are and I am grateful to each and every one of them.

Index